NATIONAL PORTRAIT GALLERY

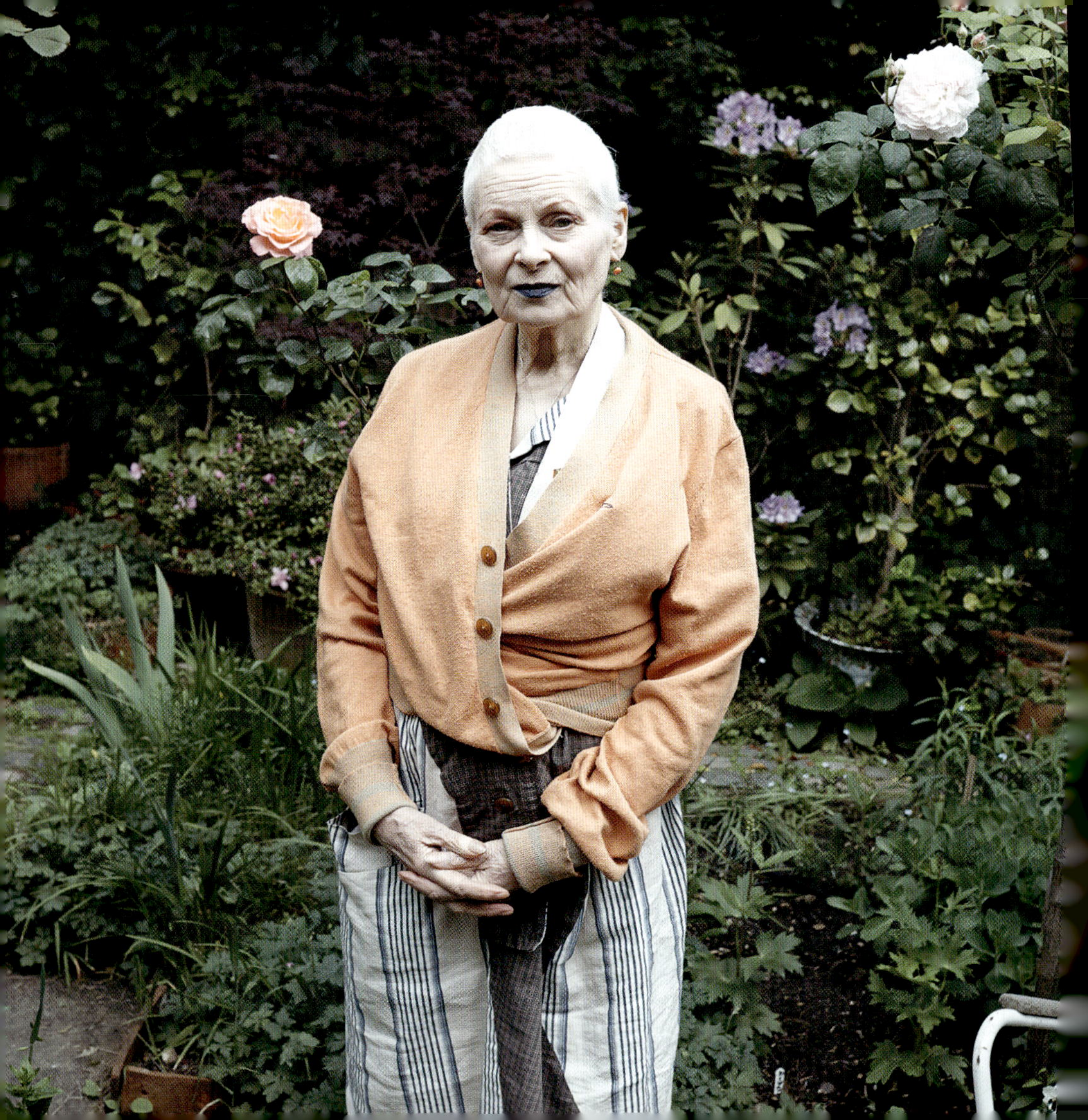

100 FASHION ICONS

CONTENTS

PAGE 2

Vivienne In Her Garden, London 2014
(DAME VIVIENNE WESTWOOD)
Juergen Teller, 2014

OPPOSITE
CAMILLE CLIFFORD
Bassano Ltd, 1906

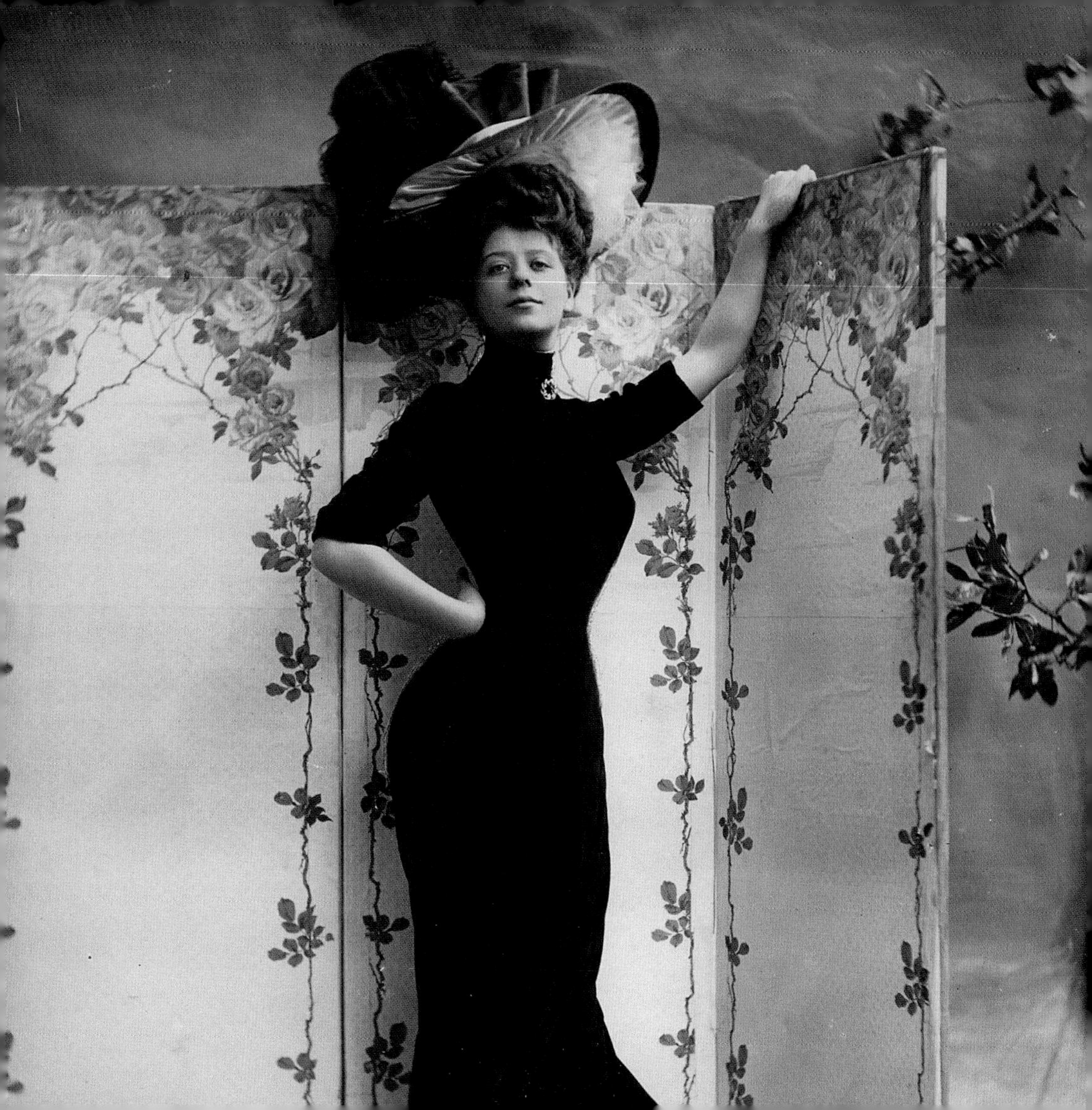

INTRODUCTION
MAGDA KEANEY

Portraits are an encounter between history, biography and art. If this selection of one hundred images from the collection of the National Portrait Gallery, London, demonstrates one thing, it is that very often fashion is also integral to this creative collaboration. In art, as in life, fashion brings style, glamour and beauty to the party, embellishing the barest studio setting or otherwise unadorned sitter through the magnificence of fabrics and design, the intricacy of jewellery you can't take your eyes off, or the idiosyncrasies of hairstyling or make-up of a particular period.

The Gallery's collection includes portraits of those who have made fashion: significant designers, editors and photographers whose vision and innovation have shaped not only what is worn, but also our perception of the aesthetic sensibilities of an era. It includes photographs that illustrate fashion styles and are often highlights from the history of fashion image-making. Such portraits combine noteworthy sitters, cutting-edge designs and the most important photographers of the time. The Collection also features fashion photographs of sitters who were considered fashion icons of their age and who – combining elements of fame (or infamy), individuality and sartorial flair –

have inspired and influenced fashion, hair and make-up trends and expanded the definitions of beauty while sometimes also challenging mainstream ideals. The photographic portrait has had a particular and important dialogue with fashion and, as a result, the Photographs collection of the National Portrait Gallery holds many thousands of works that are also important fashion images – in some cases because of what is worn, the person who wears it or the person who made it, and in the most exciting cases due to a rare combination of the three.

The selection of images in this publication includes a wonderful image of women making hats in the Maison Lewis by the prolific English photography studio Bassano. This is one of a small group of photographs showing the production of the hats, which complements a larger range of pictures made as publicity plates for the Parisian atelier, who had premises on Regent Street in London and whose wares were advertised as 'the smartest hats in town'.[1] Hats made with exotic animal furs are visible on the work table in the photograph – feathers were highly fashionable until the beginning of the First World War.

Portraits of fashion designers are prevalent in the Gallery collection and these include images that allude to the craft and materials behind the creation of garments, such as the contact sheet showing British set designer James Bailey and French fashion designer Pierre Balmain working with fabrics and mannequins probably in preparation for a production of the play *The Millionairess* in 1952, which starred Katharine Hepburn. Not only seen at work, designers also sat for posed studio portraits from the early decades of the twentieth century when couturiers became celebrated personalities. Such portraits often accompanied profiles in magazines including *Vogue* and *Harper's Bazaar* and served to advertise the design house and fuel the growing cultural interest in fashion, and indeed fashion photography, beyond a historically small elite. British photographer Cecil Beaton often photographed and collaborated with artists and designers for both *Vogue* commissions and also for his own books and exhibitions. He produced a profile portrait of Elsa Schiaparelli in front of a starry backdrop typical of his work of the time in terms of mood and composition. Schiaparelli wears one of her own couture designs – a white feather cape over a silk crepe gown with *trompe l'oeil* pleats painted by the artist Jean Dunand. In Beaton's image the designer is not portrayed as a maker but as a bohemian beauty.

In an equally sublime image, American photographer Deborah Turbeville was commissioned by *Vogue* to photograph designer Jean Muir as part of a series on designers and their muses. Turbeville was one of a small number of female fashion photographers working visibly during the 1970s and 1980s, and her work is significant because her images portray women as being creative, complex and independent as well as beautiful or highly sexualised. Turbeville photographed Muir in her sparsely decorated apartment across the road from the Victoria and Albert Museum in South Kensington, London, while the designer's friends modelled her clothes. Turbeville described that in this enigmatic portrait 'what you don't hear … is the sound of Ms Muir's voice … like a cricket … echoed by similar sounds of the telephones ringing throughout the apartment'.[2]

More recently British photographer Paul Wetherell photographed Christopher Bailey on the occasion of his final collection presentation as Creative Director of the iconic British fashion house Burberry for *Vogue*. Bailey is credited with refreshing the image of an establishment brand known for trench coats, reinforcing its position as a high-fashion, luxury label sought after by younger generations. Wetherell made

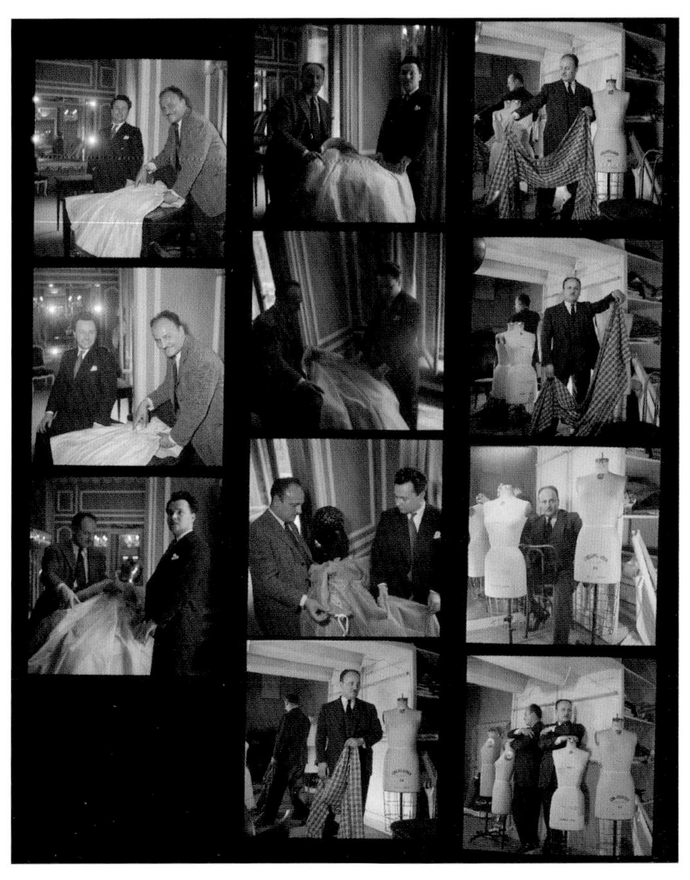

JAMES BAILEY (1925–80) and
PIERRE BALMAIN (1914–82)
Francis Goodman, 1952

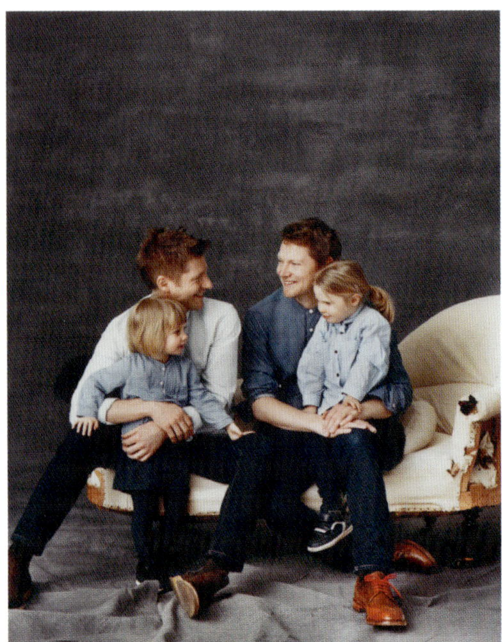

CHRISTOPHER BAILEY (b.1971)
and SIMON WOODS (b.1980) with
their daughters Nell and Iris
Paul Wetherell, 2018

an informal but intimate portrait of Bailey
with his husband, actor Simon Woods, and
their daughters, Nell and Iris; the family
appear relaxed and are dressed casually rather
than as 'fashion icons'. In the contemporary

period, fashion designers are often more
likely to make public appearances in informal
fashion rather than a collection piece. For
another image from this series, Wetherell
photographed models Cara Delevingne
and Adwoa Aboah wearing designs from
the last show celebrating LGBTQ identity,
which featured rainbow pride colours
throughout the collection.

Although what we think of as fashion
photography today emerged in the first
decade of the twentieth century, striking
fashion is integral to many nineteenth
century and early twentieth century portraits
in the Gallery collection: from the long-
sleeved, silk day dresses, lace detailing and
crinolines which featured in Camille Silvy's
photographs from the 1860s; to the
unconventional loose, billowing smock
dresses worn by Jane Morris, which set her
apart as belonging to the creative milieu of
her day; to photographs of leading ladies of
the stage such as Lillie Langtry in costumes
by the foremost designers. In contrast to these
examples, the explorers who accompanied
Captain Robert Falcon Scott to the Antarctic
in 1911 were photographed by Herbert
George Ponting wearing ribbed seafaring
woollen jumpers, knitted hats, thick trousers
and waterproof jackets. Their clothing was

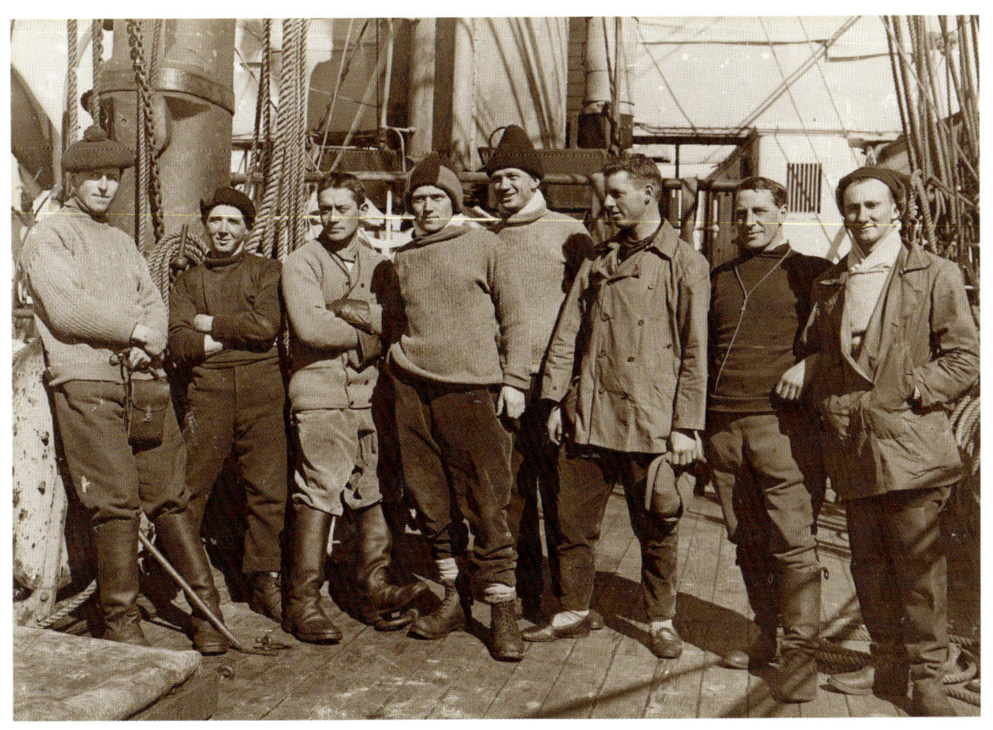

the best available at the time, yet their kit is
a world away from modern survival-wear that
has made exploration in extreme cold
considerably safer. While new technologies
have revolutionised the look, weight and
effectiveness of outdoor-wear, the clothes
seen on the explorers of the *Terra Nova*

OFFICERS OF THE *TERRA NOVA*
Herbert George Ponting, 1910

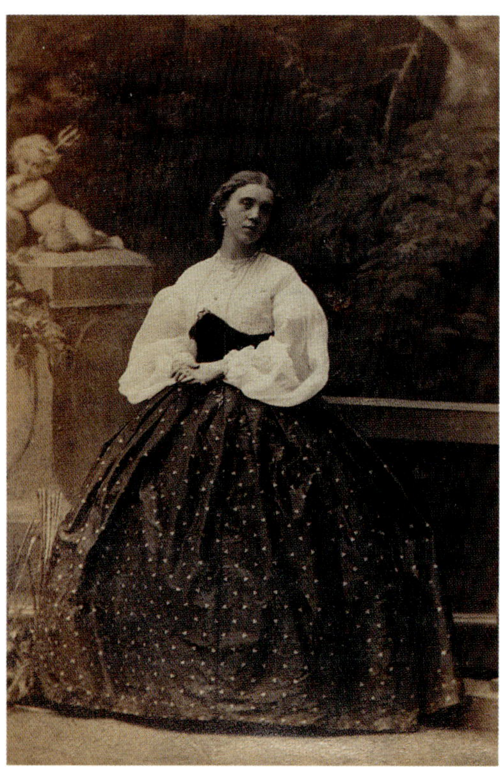

MISS FITZGERALD
(dates unknown)
Camille Silvy, 1904

have re-emerged as a fashionable style reference for contemporary menswear.

The number of portraits that were made as fashion photographs and published in magazines increased after the 1920s, many of which featured fashion models who were icons in their own right. A key early example in the Gallery collection is Cecil Beaton's 1929 photograph of Lee Miller and Marion Morehouse taken in the lavish surroundings of Condé Nast's penthouse apartment in New York. As the owner of *Vogue*, Nast had transformed the application of photography in the illustration of fashion. The double portrait shows Miller and Morehouse, two of the most sought-after models of the day, posing in matching dresses and jewellery. The image is significant as it charts the development of both the professional fashion photographer as well as the fashion model. Nast's apartment was a de facto photography studio and provided the setting for the illustration of new designs, which previously had taken place in the commercial photographic studio setting. Nast soon after established studios especially for the making of fashion images such as this and helped establish stylistic conventions that would take hold and characterise fashion photography for most of the twentieth century.

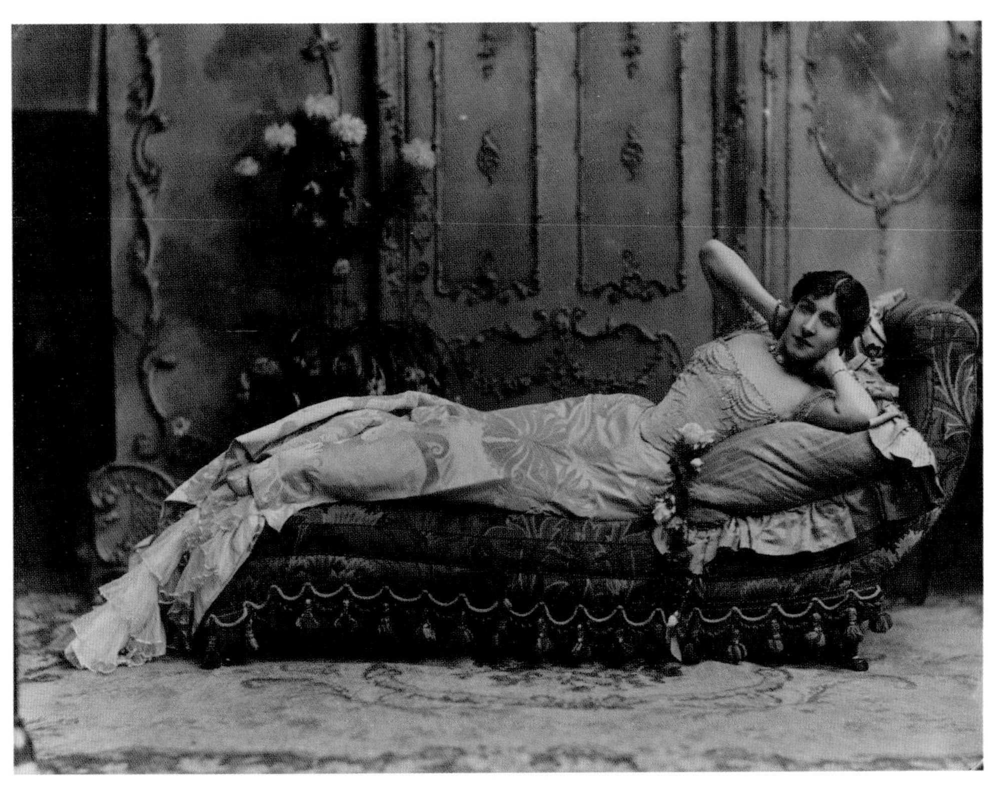

LILLIE LANGTRY (1853–1929)

Lafayette, 1899

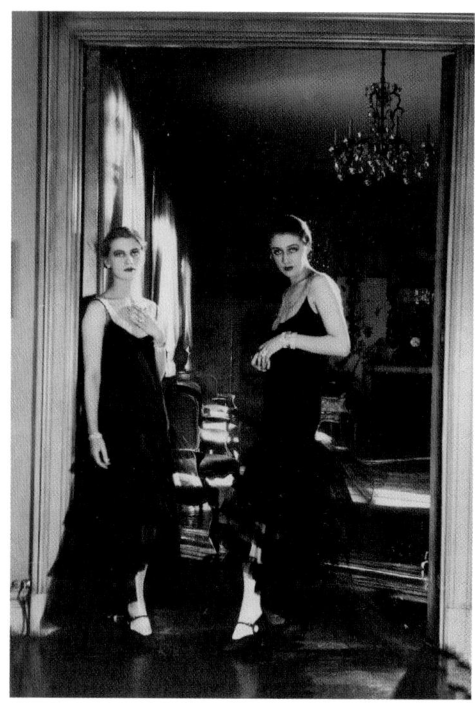

Photography is the medium that, beyond other genres of portraiture, has in fact enabled the very notion of the fashion icon. Although fashion icons are represented in painted portraits, it is the reproducibility as well as the immediacy of photography that has made it well-suited to the depiction of personalities collectively admired as enduringly fashionable. Some sitters have become fashion icons unwittingly or in the process of simply conducting their lives in the public eye. Perhaps the royal family is the best example of this, whose portraits have been made tirelessly since the invention of photography. Queen Alexandra, the wife of Edward VII, was photographed by Symonds & Co in August 1880 on board the Royal Yacht *Osborne* typically well dressed, including a straw hat and a fitted buttoned-and-belted jacket with cuffs and collar details, which matches Charles Dickens' description of her as having 'a character distinctive of her own, prepared to act a part greatly'.[3] An amateur photographer, Queen Alexandra was also the subject of the most popular *carte-de-visite* portraits of the day. Wallis, Duchess of Windsor, was also certainly a fashion icon. She embraced feted Parisian designers including Schiaparelli, Dior, Givenchy and Mainbocher. In 2012, French designer Roland Mouret included

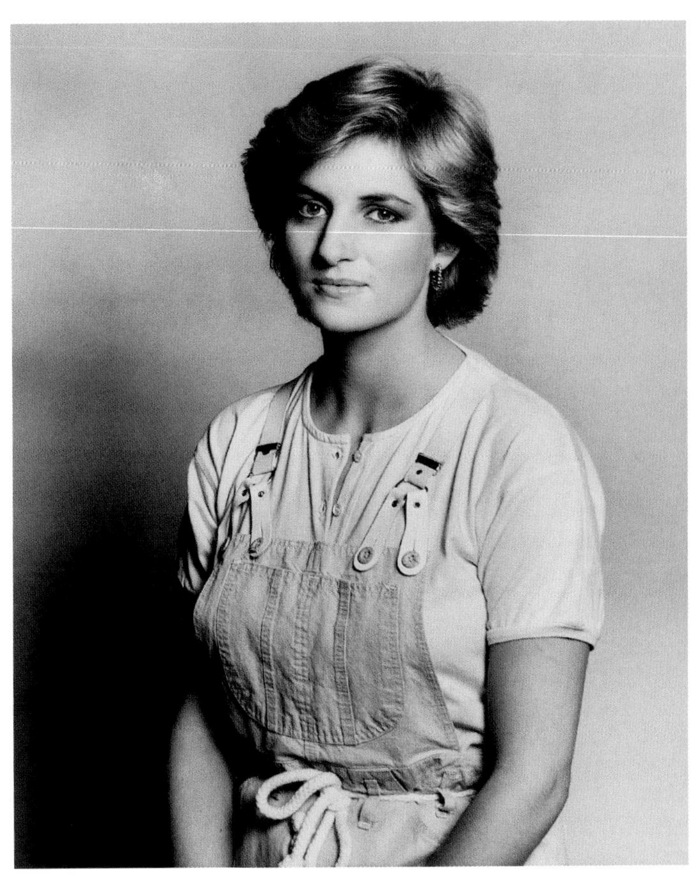

DIANA, PRINCESS OF WALES
(1961–97)
Terence Donovan, 1986

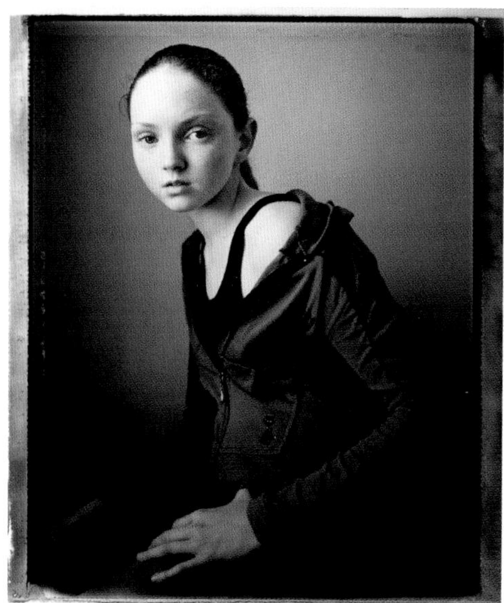

LILY COLE (b.1987)
Mariano Vivanco, 2001

woman transformed into a princess and later as a glamourous stateswoman, an ambassador for humanitarian aid and a devoted mother.

Popular culture has also supplied an ample number of portraits to the Gallery collection in which a fashionable element is now often expected. A portrait of Madonna is almost always also a fashion statement, set to be both a barometer of when it was made and often in retrospect relatable to a particular period of music made by her. An unmistakably eighties image taken by Eric Watson for a cover feature in the music magazine *Smash Hits* is now instantly associated with her early career and breakthrough first album, and speaks to the danceclub scene of the 1980s featured in her first music video for the song 'Everybody' (1983). In the portrait, she wears an oversized jumper and matching socks paired with a graphic Keith Haring skirt (Madonna and Haring were close friends), accessorised with the layering of bangles, necklaces and crosses for which she was known in that decade. In a recent example, London-based photographer Olivia Rose created a portrait of the grime artist Stormzy wearing an Adidas tracksuit and trademark socks and slides. Sportswear brands such as Nike and Adidas have been popularised by celebrities worldwide.

a gold, embossed silk maxi-dress inspired by the Duchess for his autumn/winter collection saying, 'Love or hate her, the world is still obsessed by that woman.'[4] Similarly, whenever Diana, Princess of Wales, was photographed or painted, her inherent sense of style and love of fashion was a distinctive characteristic, initially as part of the narrative of an ordinary young

Stormzy's fondness for the combination of socks and slides is well known and even a topic of discussion in a video interview with the musician Ed Sheeran for Noisey in 2017.[5] In 2018, Stormzy collaborated with Adidas on a 1990s and 2000s inspired collection.

It will come as no surprise that many of the most-loved photographs in the Collection are musicians, actors and models who are also fashion icons. With such large holdings it is possible to see the evolution of style across a number of significant fashion figures – for example the transformation of The Beatles from the 'mop-topped', mod look deeply connected to British working-class culture, to psychedelia and Indian-inspired fashions – or to find one of the first portraits of fashion model and actor Lily Cole aged thirteen by Mariano Vivanco alongside a portrait of her made only four years later by Miles Aldridge, transformed into the embodiment of the muse. By this time, Cole had been honoured as model of the year and was sought after for international fashion campaigns and editorials.

While fashion in its broadest sense is an element of almost every portrait, this book illustrates the indisputable potential of fashion to transform the portrait from the austere or commonplace into the definitive and spectacular. Though some commentators may debate fashion's status as art, one thing seems clear: great fashion can make a great portrait. Likewise, fashion and dress have important work to do within the portrait, providing essential clues about the person represented and expressing the complexity of individuality and identity in ways that can be subtle as well as extravagant. It was Oscar Wilde who once quipped, 'One should either be a work of art or wear a work of art.'[6] Here, then, are one hundred men and women from the Gallery collection who do both.

MAGDA KEANEY
Senior Curator, Photographs,
National Portrait Gallery, London

NOTES

1   'Fashion's Entente', *The Times*, 22 March 1923. Publication section: Advertising.

2   Deborah Turbeville, *The Fashion Pictures* (Rizzoli, New York, 2011), p.59.

3   Quoted in *Camera Portraits* (National Portrait Gallery, London, 1989), p.100.

4   Roland Mouret quoted in Imogen Fox, Anne Sebba, 'Wallis Simpson used fashion as a weapon', *Guardian*, 2 September 2011.

5   Video interview, 'Stormzy x Ed Sheeran: Back & Forth', *Noisey*, 21 Febuary, 2017. Accessed 2 June 2019, www.vice.com.

6   Oscar Wilde, *Epigrams & Aphorisms* (John Luce and Company, Boston, 1905), p.67.

MAKING FASHION

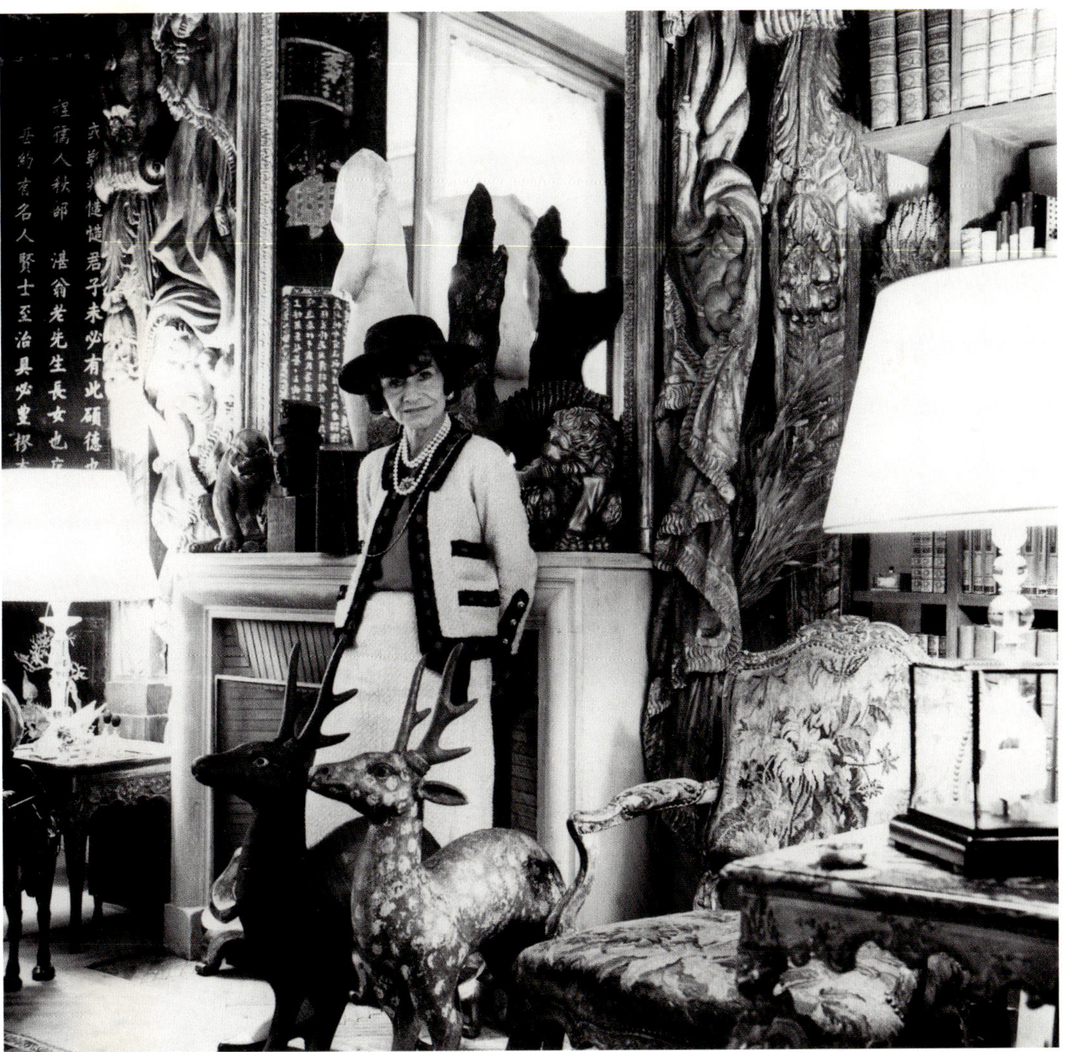

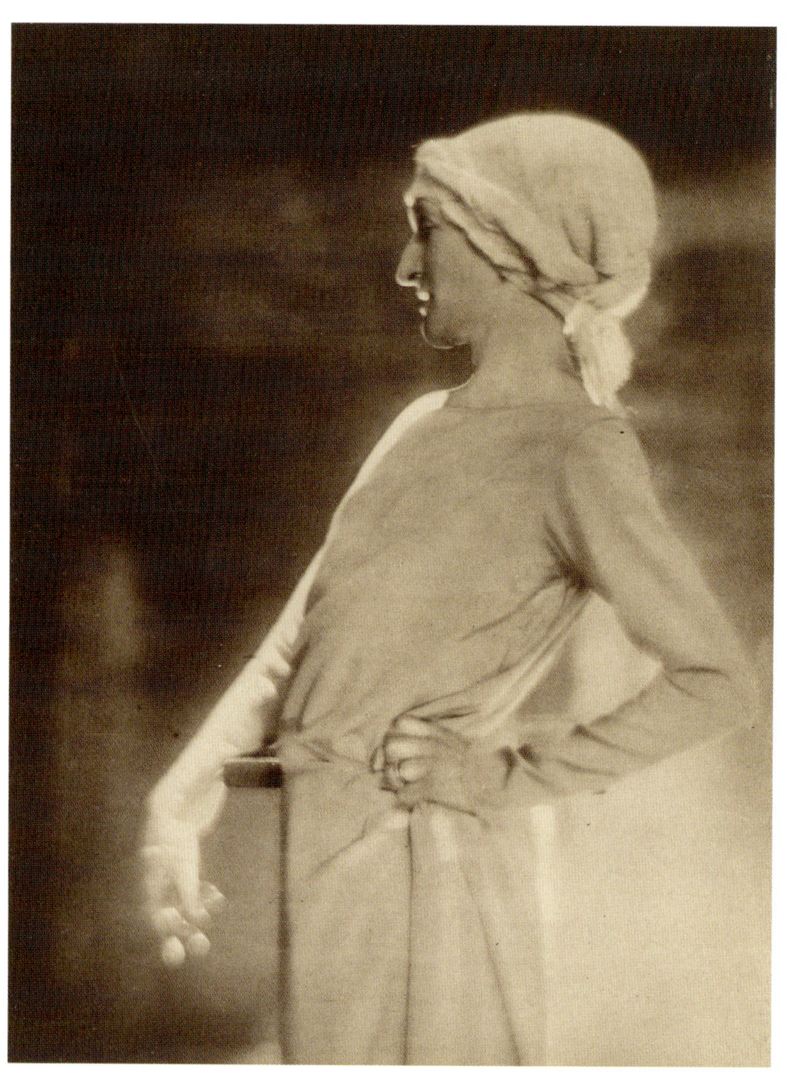

COCO CHANEL (1883–1971)

Cecil Beaton, 1965

Gelatin silver print, 194 x 195mm

NPG x40051

MARGOT ASQUITH (1864–1945)

Baron Adolph de Meyer, 1922

Gelatin silver print, 464 x 334mm

NPG P165

Margot Asquith, Countess of Oxford and Asquith, is seen here wearing a Shetland shawl tied around her head, a fashion she adopted for when she was writing. This photograph was published at the time of the launch of her book, *My Impressions of America*. German-born Baron de Meyer (1868–1946), known in London for his pictorialist work, moved to New York in 1913 to take up a post as the first staff photographer at Condé Nast, working for *Vogue* and *Vanity Fair*. In 1922, he became chief photographer for *Harper's Bazaar*. In this portrait, de Meyer styles Asquith as a romanticised, poetic figure and his use of pictorial techniques gives the portrait an ethereal quality.

MILLINERY WORKROOMS, MAISON LEWIS

Bassano Ltd, 1910

Whole-plate glass negative

NPG x104161

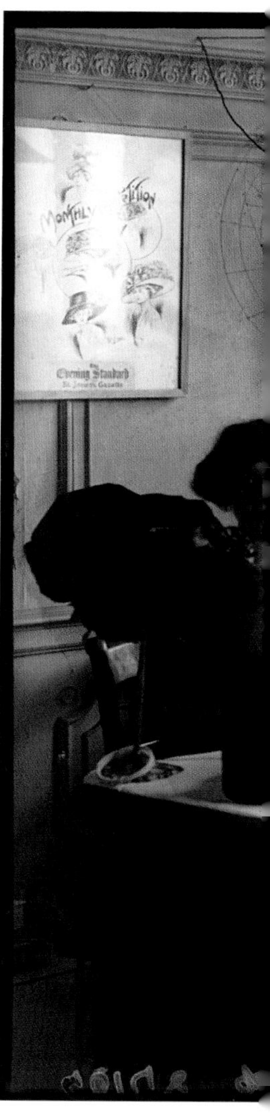

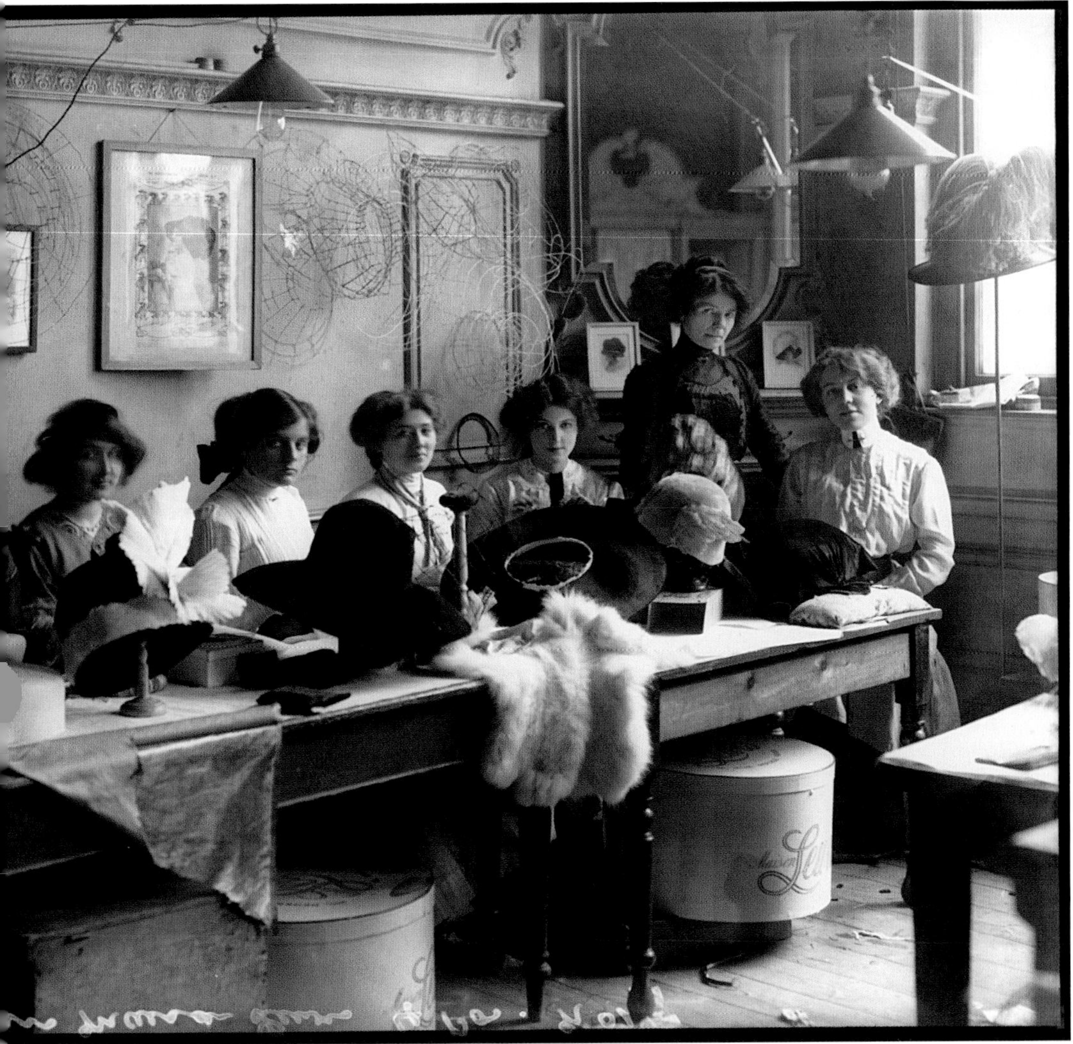

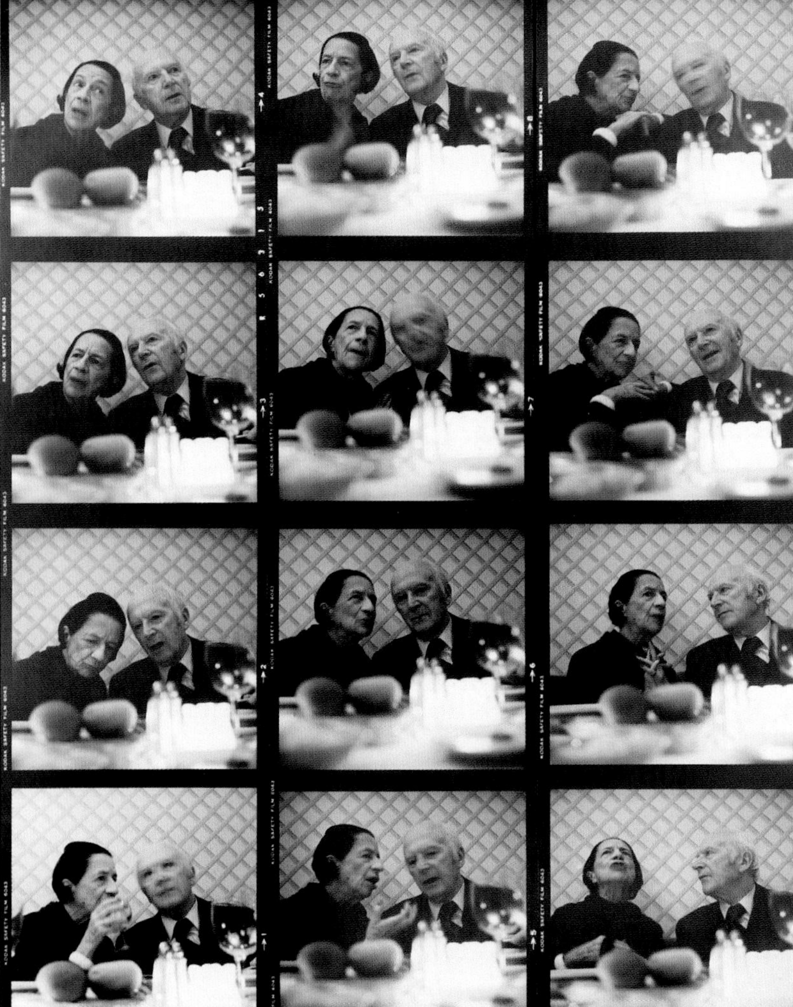

DIANA VREELAND (1901–89)
and SIR CECIL BEATON (1904–80)
James Berry, 1977–8
Gelatin silver contact print, 494 x 378mm
NPG x136051

ELSA SCHIAPARELLI

(1890–1973)

Cecil Beaton, 1936

Gelatin silver print, 237 x 191mm

NPG x40358

Elsa Schiaparelli was a leading fashion designer in the interwar period. In 1924, she established her fashion house in Paris, taking a unique approach to traditional fabrics. She described her profession as an art form, with Surrealism a main influence. Her fashion house expanded to London in 1933 and one of her frequent collaborators was society photographer Cecil Beaton (1904–80). In this photograph, Schiaparelli wears one of her 1931 haute couture creations: a white feather cape worn over a silk crêpe gown with *trompe l'oeil* pleats painted by artist Jean Dunand (1877–1942), complementing Beaton's star-printed backdrop.

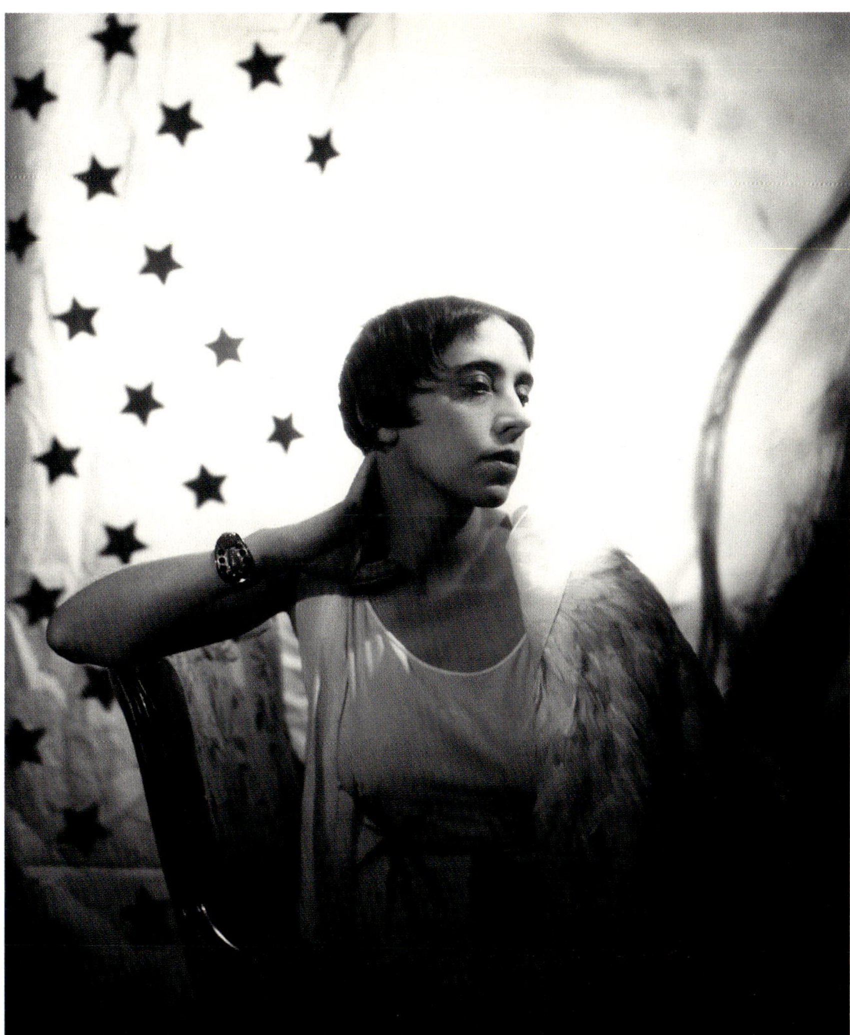

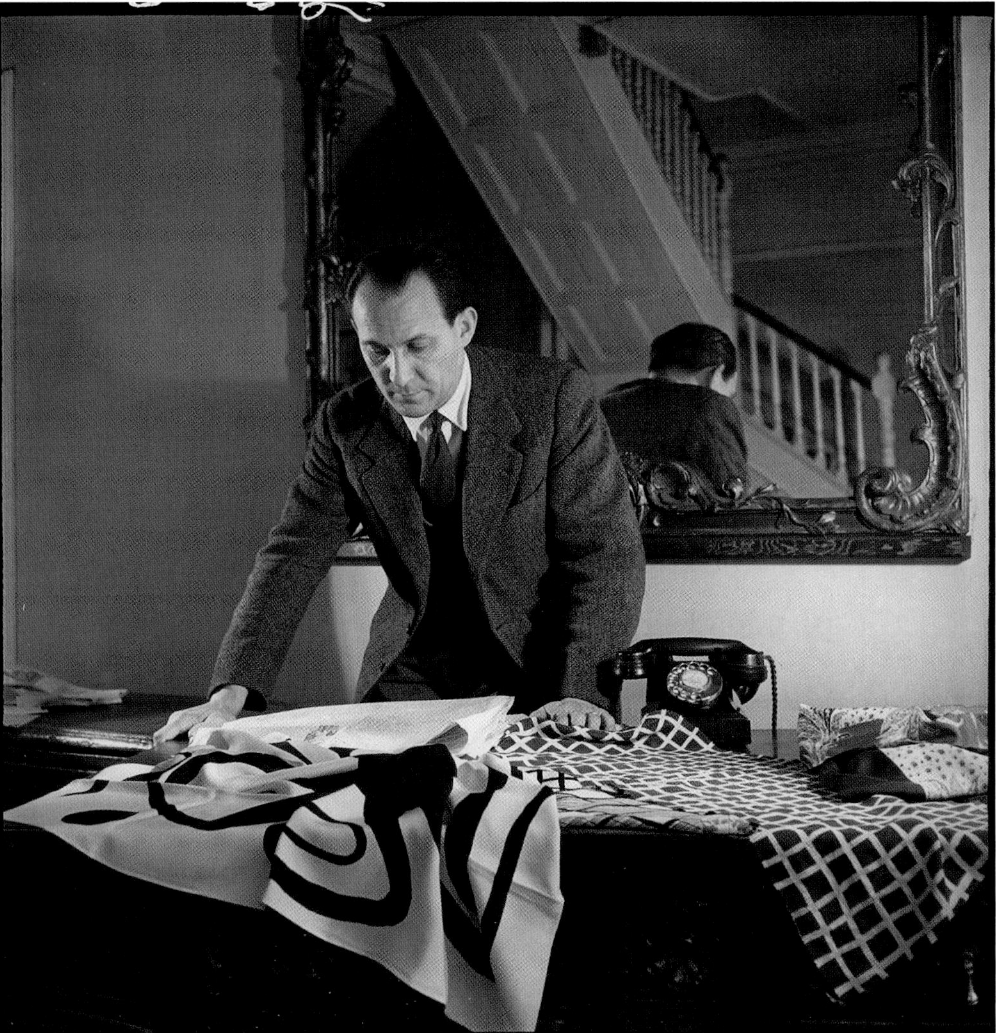

OPPOSITE
ZIKA ASCHER (1910–92)
John Gay, 1949
2 ¼ inch square film negative
NPG x128696

BELOW
LEE MILLER (1907–77)
Self-portrait, 1932
Modern gelatin silver print, 153 x 191mm
NPG P1081

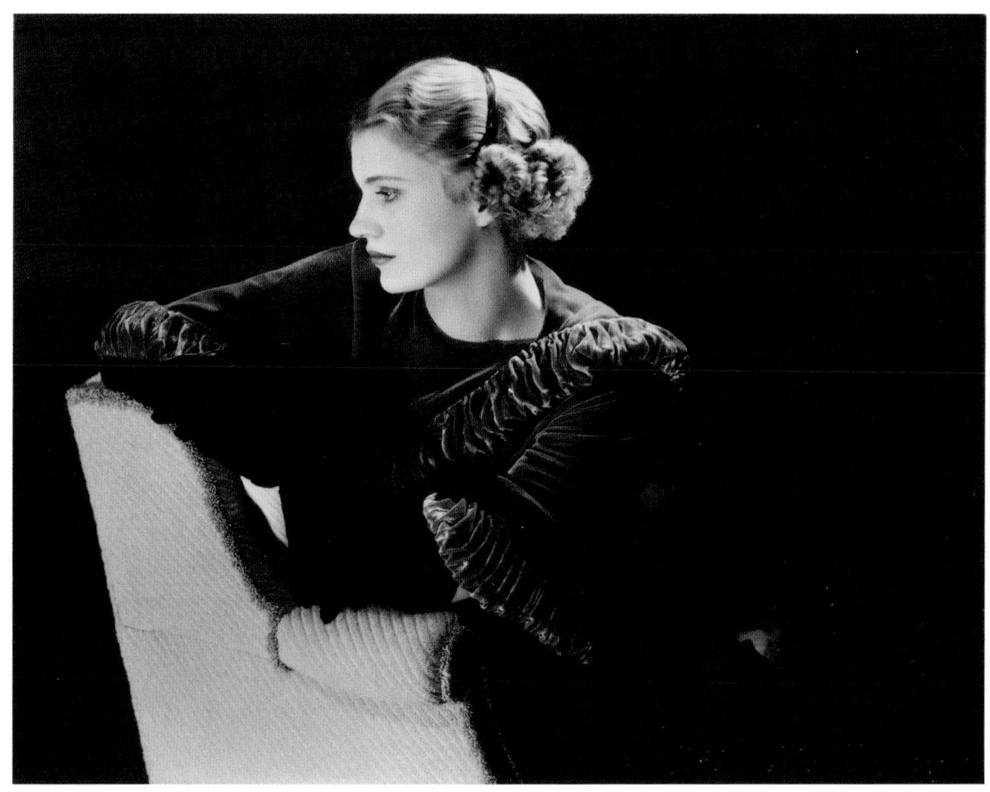

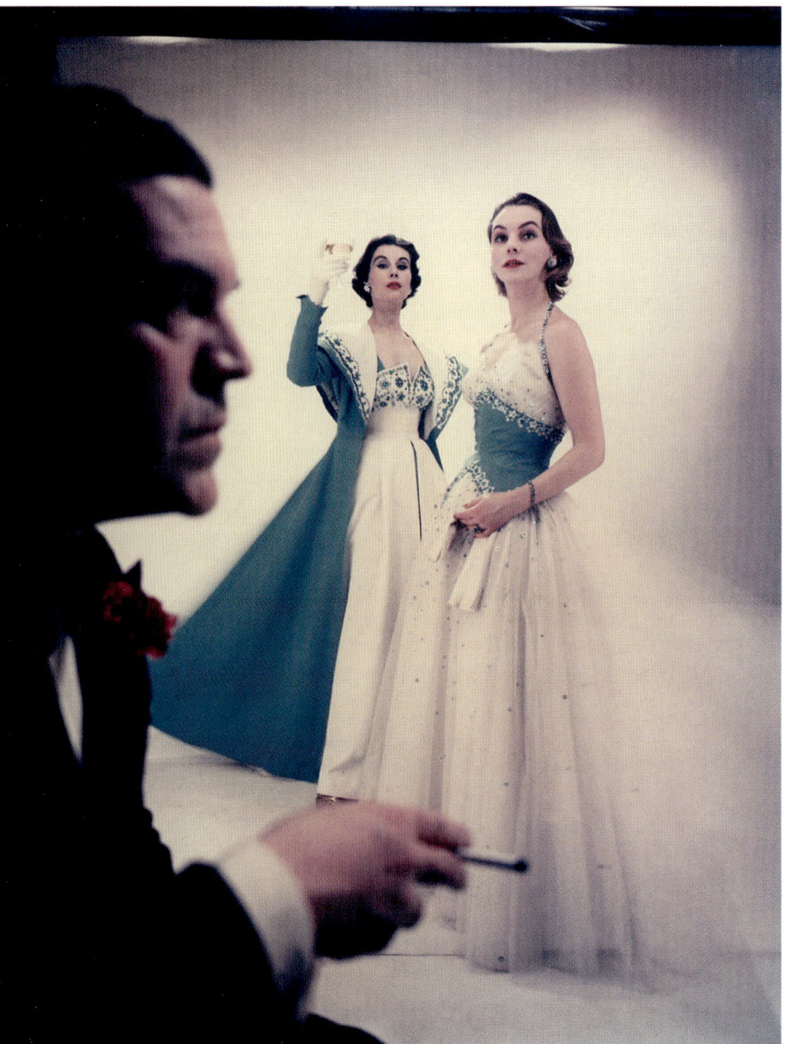

SIR NORMAN HARTNELL
(1901–79), MYRTLE CRAWFORD,
LADY ACLAND (1928–2013)
and MARGARET PHILLIPS
(dates unknown)
Norman Parkinson, 1953
Chromogenic print, 364 x 282mm
NPG x30054

Couturier Norman Hartnell opened his
first salon in 1923 and it became a landmark
in British fashion, re-establishing traditions
of hand-tailoring. Hartnell went on to create
both Queen Elizabeth II's wedding dress
and coronation gown. In this photograph
by celebrated fashion photographer Norman
Parkinson (1913–90), Hartnell poses with
models Myrtle Crawford and Margaret
Phillips wearing his gowns for a *Vogue* issue
published in March 1953. Working for
Harper's Bazaar, *Vogue*, *Queen* and *Town &
Country*, Parkinson's innovative shoots
involving storytelling and glamour were
most often taken outside of the studio.

BELOW
CAROLINE CHARLES (b.1942)
Allan Ballard, 1960s
Gelatin silver print, 232 x 356mm
NPG X125460

OPPOSITE
JOHN STEPHEN (1934–2004)
Angela Williams, 1960s
Cibachrome print, 395 x 257mm
NPG X125457

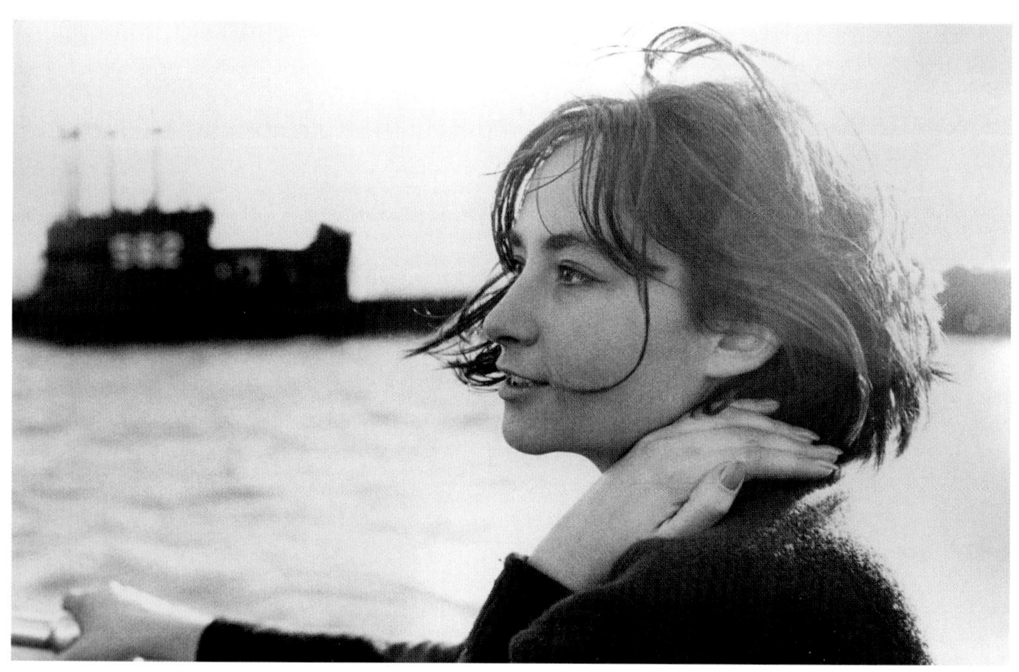

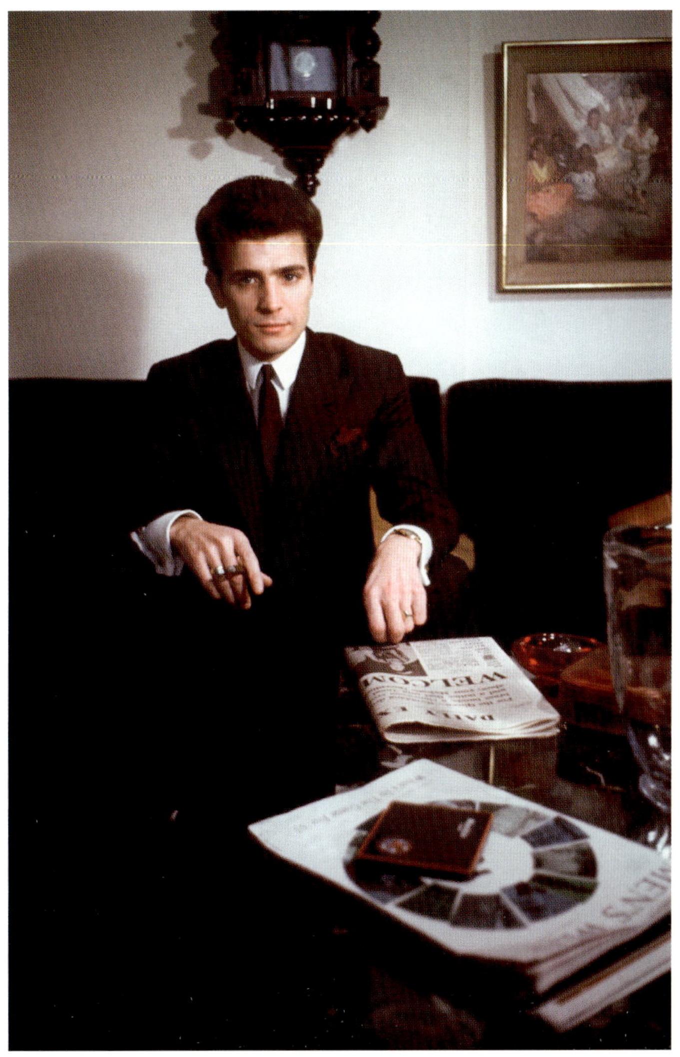

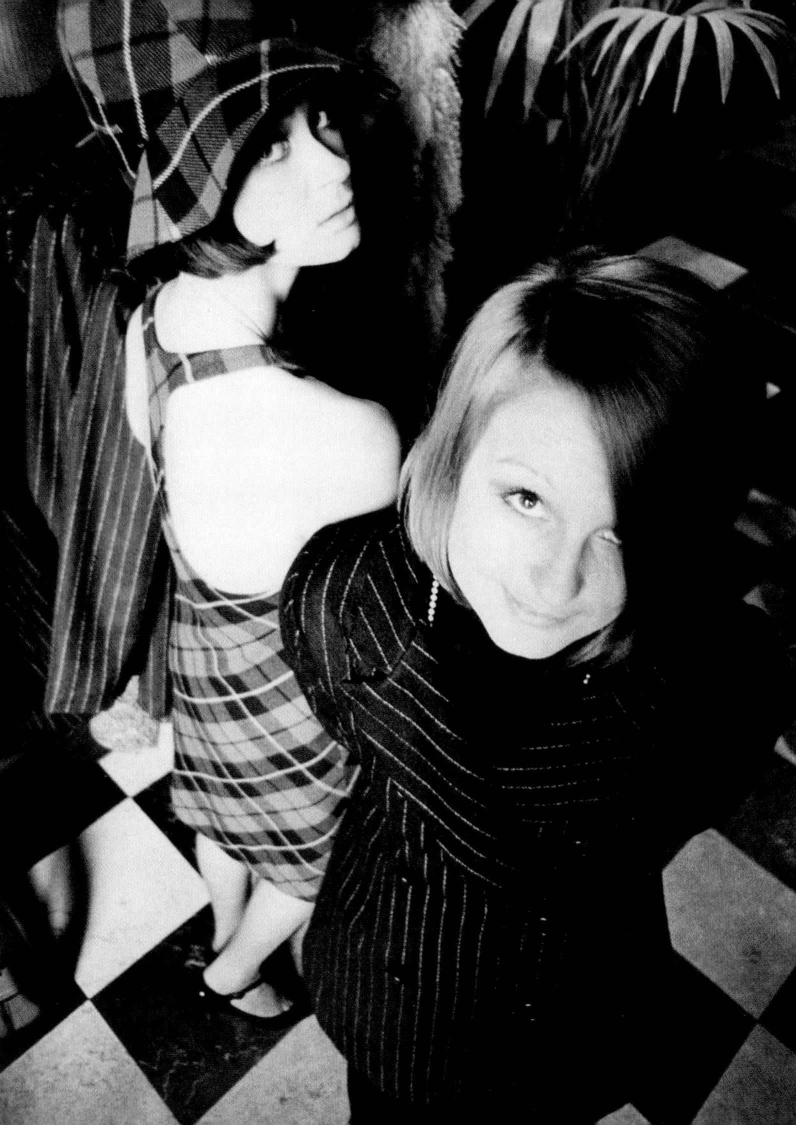

OPPOSITE
BARBARA HULANICKI (b.1936)
with model
Harri Peccinotti, 1965
Gelatin silver print, 478 x 325mm
NPG x199146

RIGHT
GRACE CODDINGTON (b.1941)
Eric Swayne, 1966
Gelatin silver print, 553 x 376mm
NPG x135471

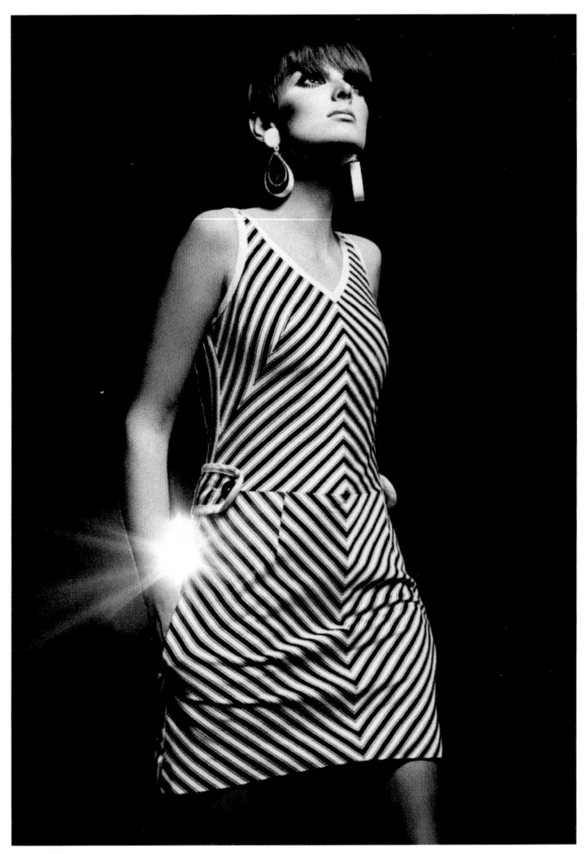

DAME MARY QUANT (b.1934),
ALEXANDER PLUNKET
GREENE (1932–90) and nine models
(*A Crate Full of Quant*)
John Adriaan, 1966
Gelatin silver print, 459 x 358mm
NPG x133068

Fashion designer Dame Mary Quant
opened her first Bazaar boutique on
King's Road in Chelsea, London, in 1955.
She married her work partner, the fashion
entrepreneur Alexander Plunket Greene,
in 1957. Quant became known for her bold,
geometric designs and for popularising
the miniskirt, which became synonymous
with the 'Swinging Sixties' in London.
Photographer John Adriaan's image for
the *Daily Mirror* – featuring models Vicky
Hodge, Peggy Moffitt, Linda Carlens,
Jenny Fassell, Karina, Renate, Jill Wight,
Lorraine Chase and Sarah Dawson –
celebrates the imminent worldwide
launch of Quant's cosmetics line, which
joined her vastly successful underwear and
outerwear ranges. All Quant products were
branded with the classic daisy logo.

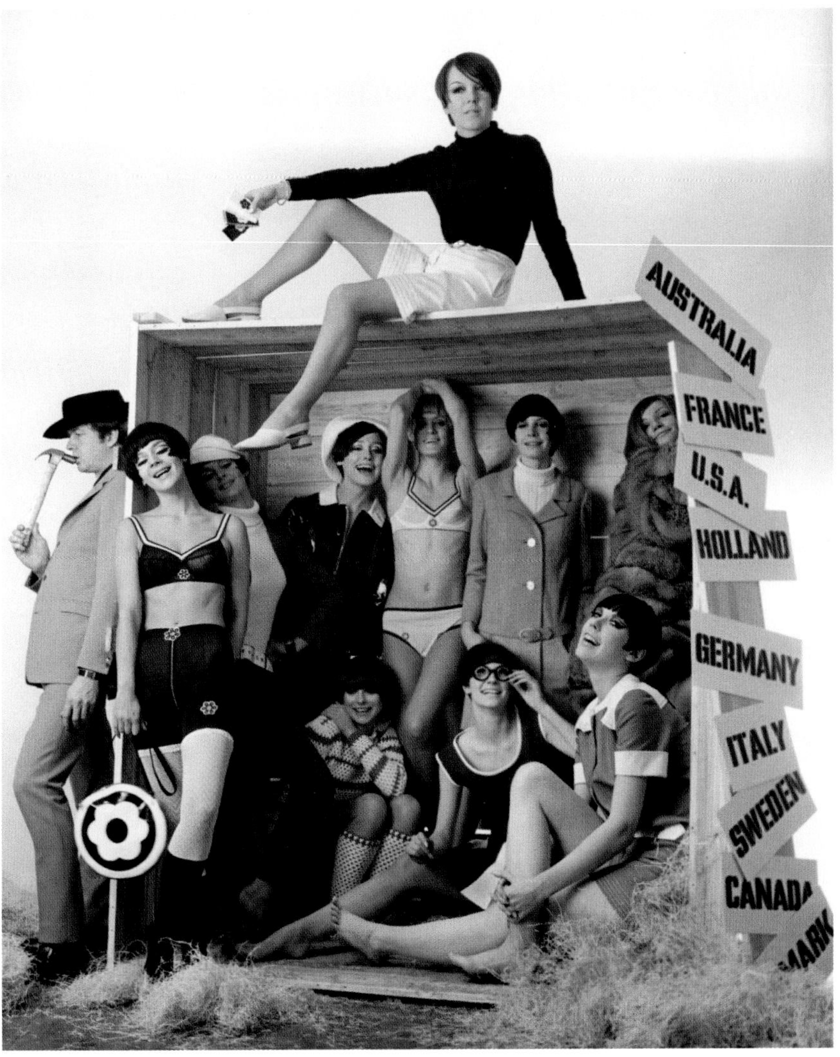

AUSTRALIA
FRANCE
U.S.A.
HOLLAND
GERMANY
ITALY
SWEDEN
CANADA
MARK

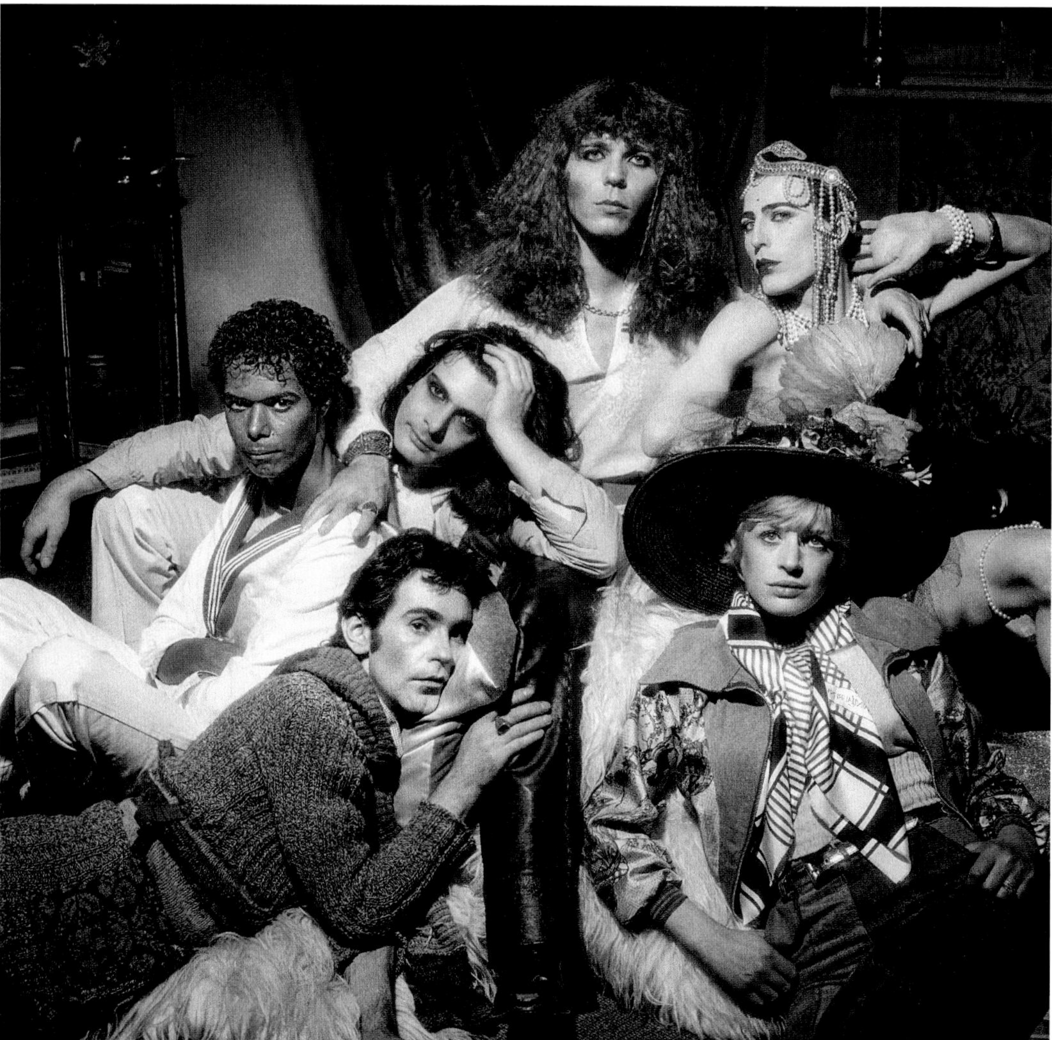

MICHAEL ROBERTS (b.1947),
OSSIE CLARK (1942–96), MICKEY
FINN (1947–2003), PIERRE LA
ROCHE (1931–2014), VALENTINO
MOON (dates unknown) and
MARIANNE FAITHFULL (b.1946)
Clive Arrowsmith, 1973
Chromogenic print, 443 x 442mm
NPG x199703

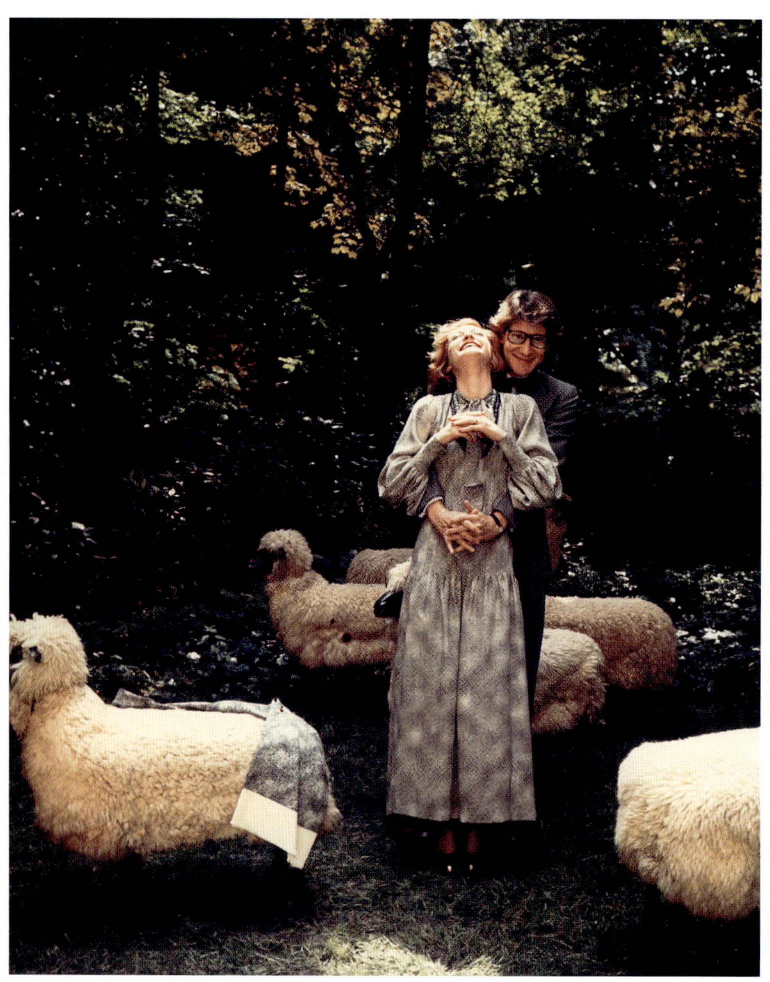

    100 FASHION ICONS

OPPOSITE
LOULOU DE LA FALAISE
(1948–2011) and YVES SAINT
LAURENT (1936–2008)
Norman Parkinson, 1974
Colour coupler print, 394 x 378mm
NPG x30157

RIGHT
LAURA ASHLEY (1925–85)
Robin Laurance, 1977
Gelatin silver print, 470 x 310mm
NPG x128606

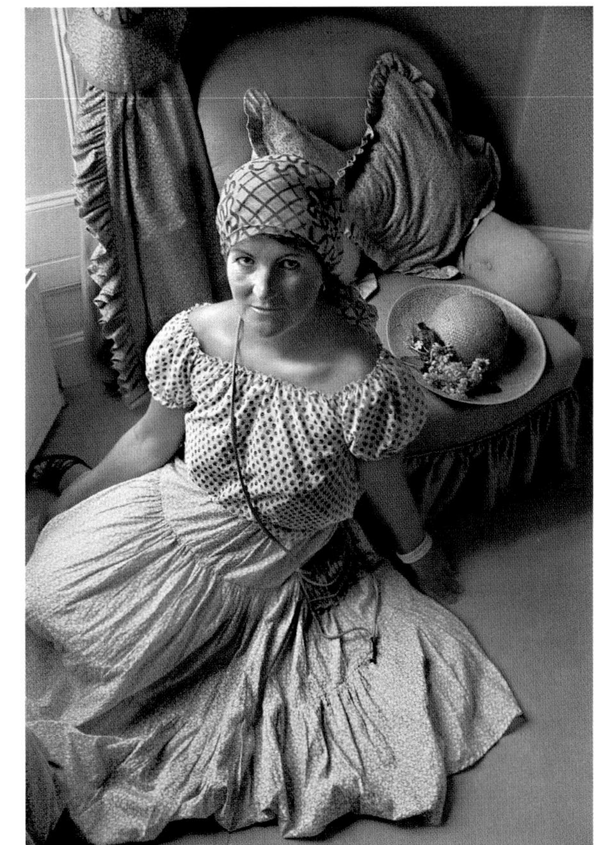

CALVIN KLEIN (b.1942)

Horst P. Horst, 1984

Chromogenic print, 288 x 291mm

NPG x137754

JEAN PAUL GAULTIER (b.1952)

Angus McBean, 1988

Chromogenic print, 210 x 178mm

NPG x128898

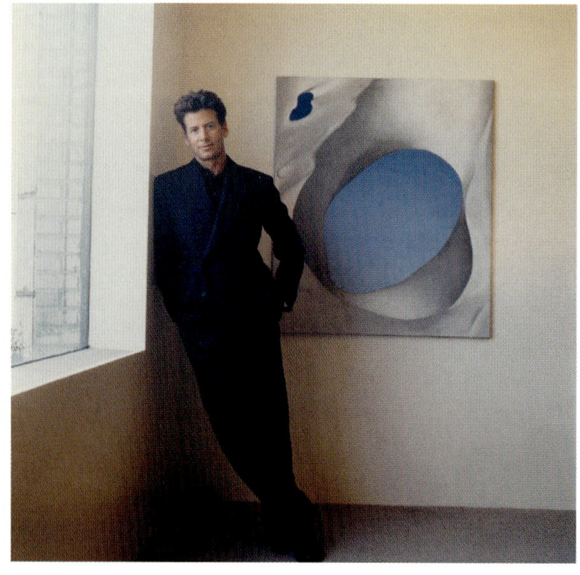

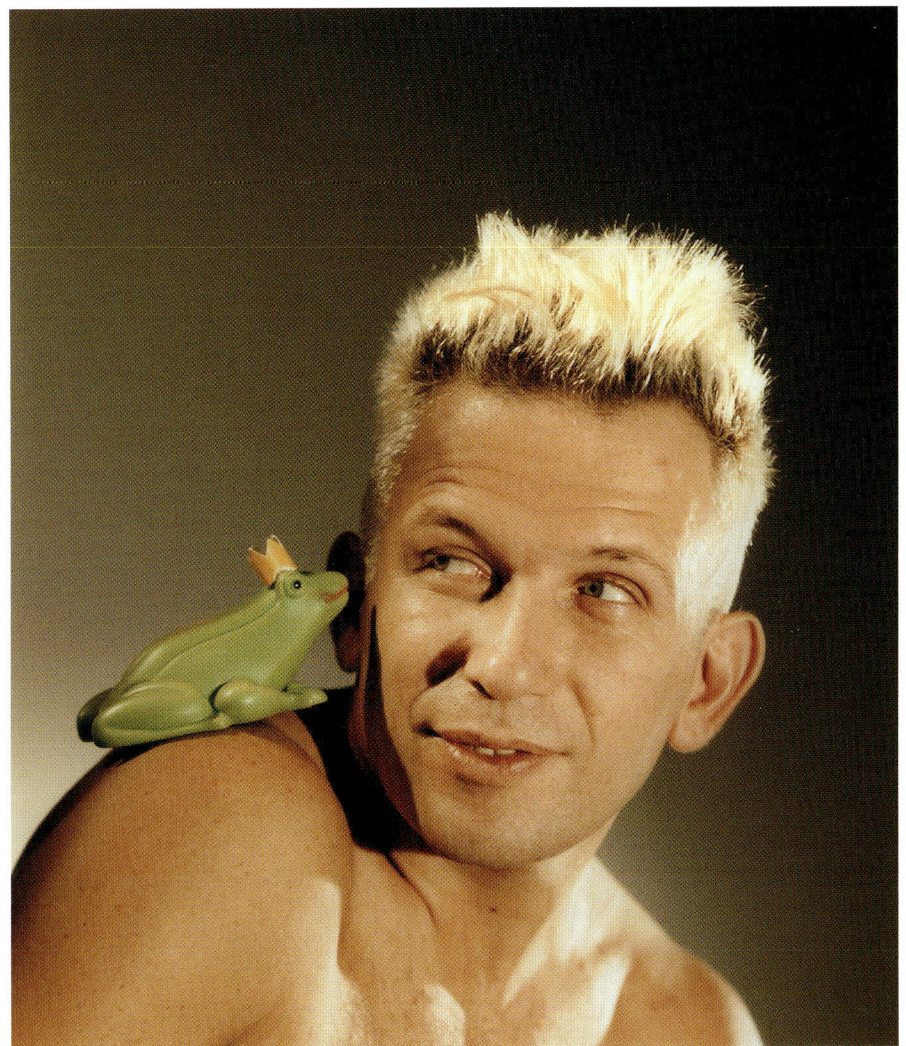

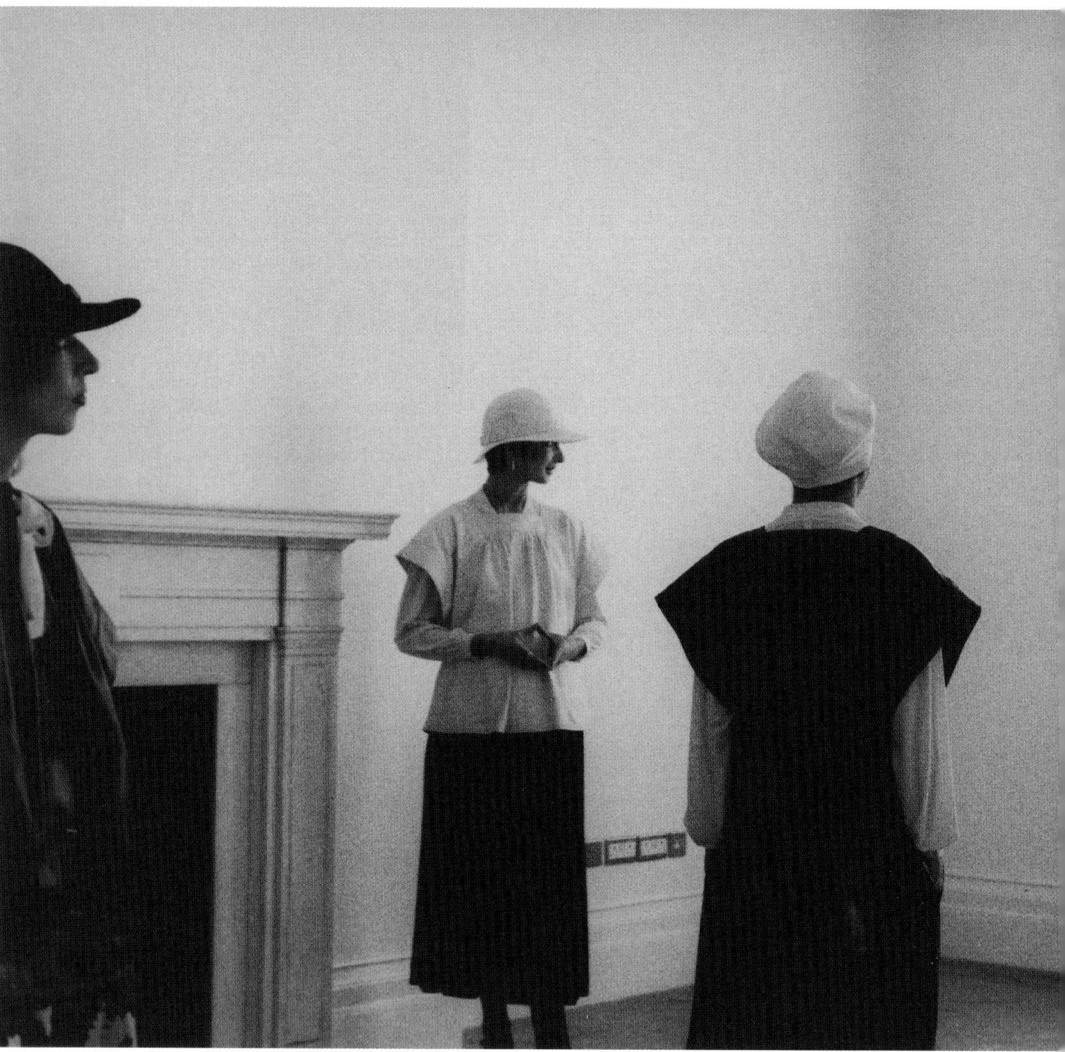

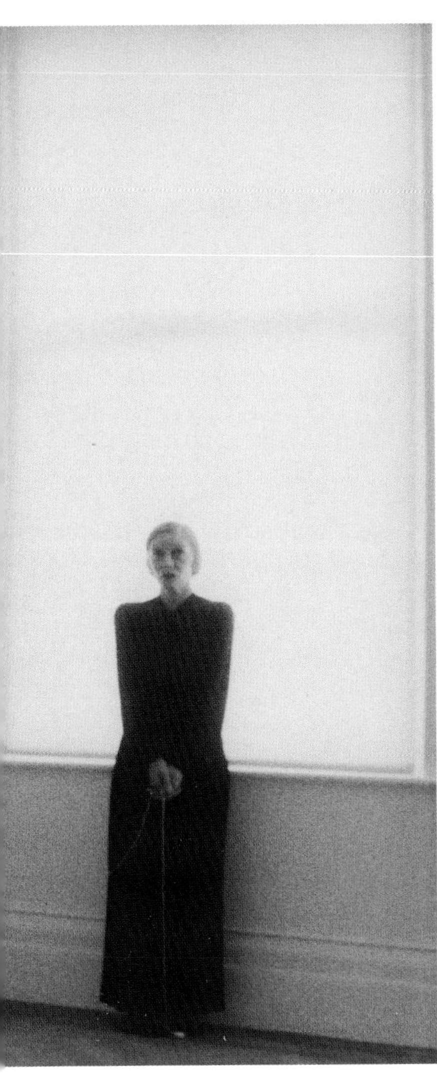

JEAN MUIR (1928–95) and three
models
Deborah Turbeville, 1980s
Gelatin silver print, 356 x 508mm
NPG P2033

Fashion designer Jean Muir was famed
for the classic cut and simplicity of her
garments. Muir worked for the fashion
brand Jaeger during the 1950s, forming
Jean Muir Limited with her husband
Harry Leuckert in 1966. American
photographer Deborah Turbeville
(1932–2013) began her career in fashion
in the editorial departments of *Mademoiselle*
and *Harper's Bazaar* before taking up
photography in the 1960s. Turbeville
challenged the highly objectified aesthetic
of her male contemporaries through
mysterious and evocative compositions.
Muir's virtually empty London flat
provides the blank canvas for the
formation of Muir's friends wearing her
clothes, with the designer herself backlit
against the window.

STEPHEN JONES (b.1957)
Nick Knight, 1985
Gelatin silver print, 550 x 457mm
NPG x26091

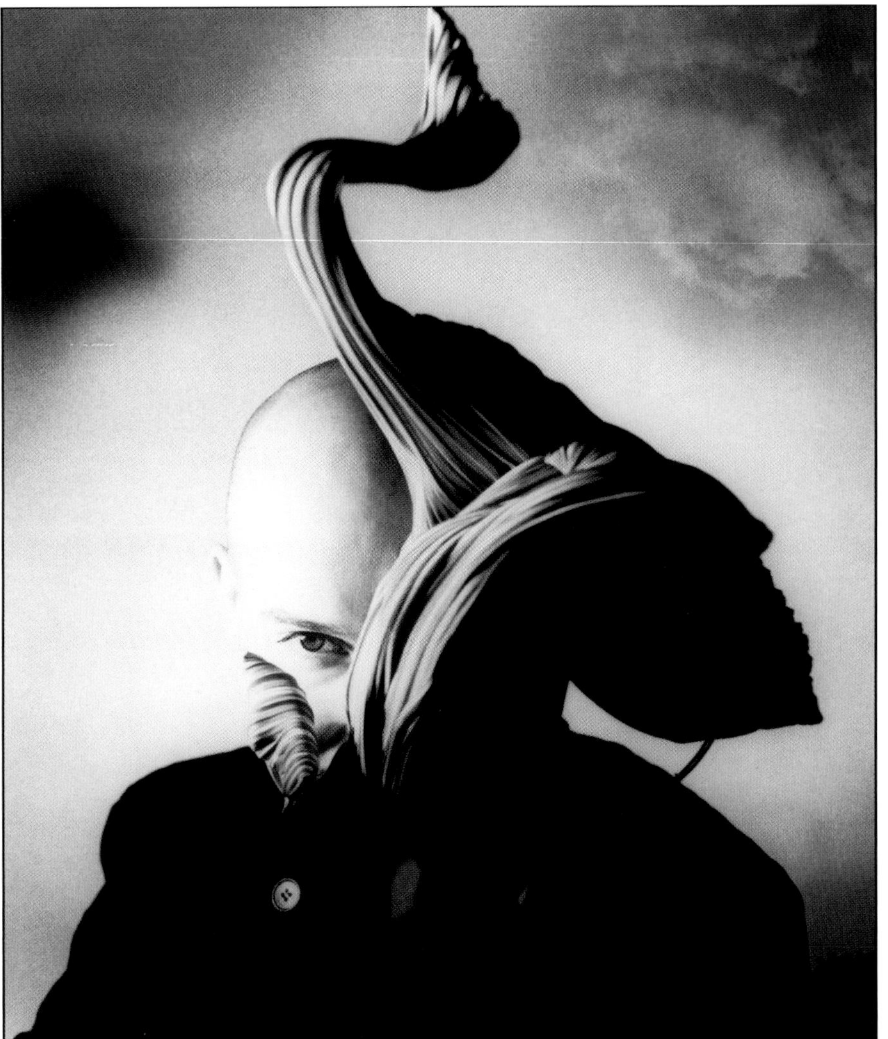

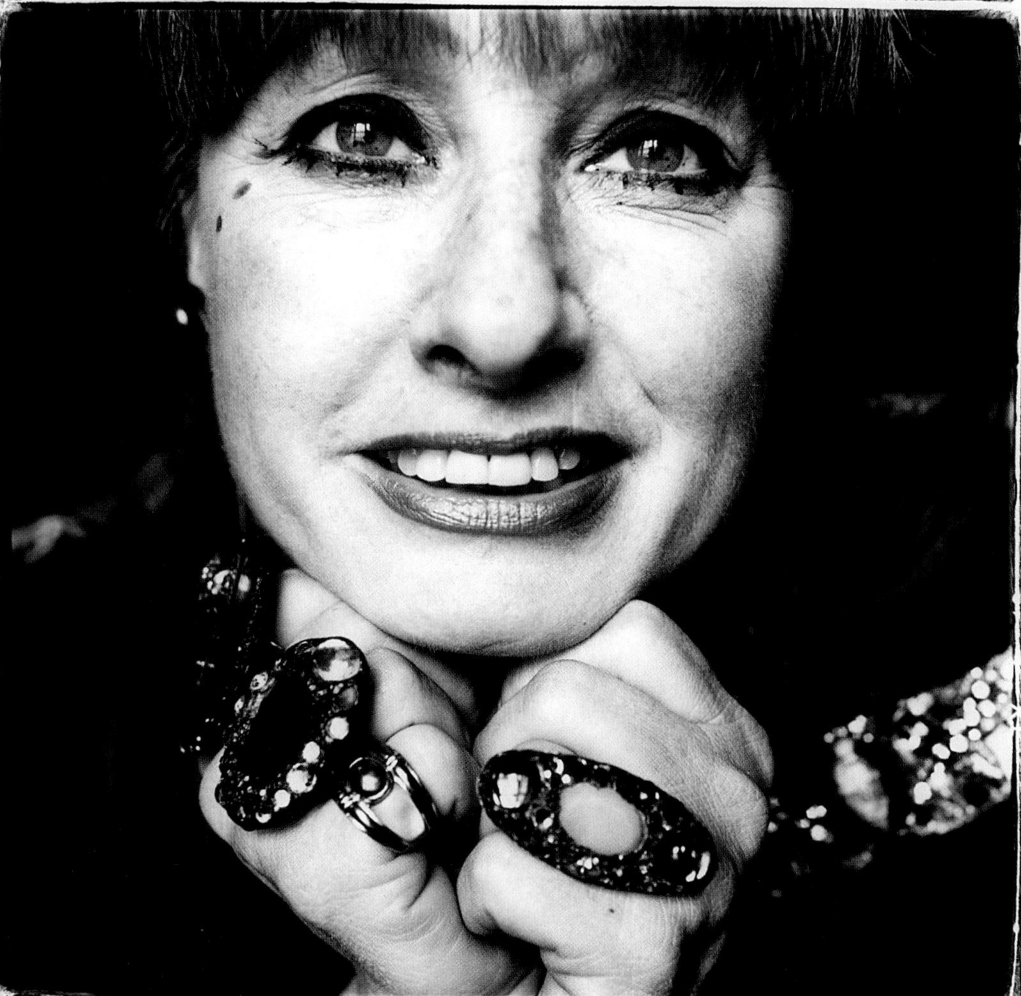

OPPOSITE
DAME ZANDRA RHODES
(b.1940)
Steve Pyke, 1993
Gelatin silver print, 266 x 268mm
NPG x45581

RIGHT
ALEXANDRA SHULMAN
(b.1957)
Jane Bown, 1996
Gelatin silver print, 347 x 238mm
NPG x88792

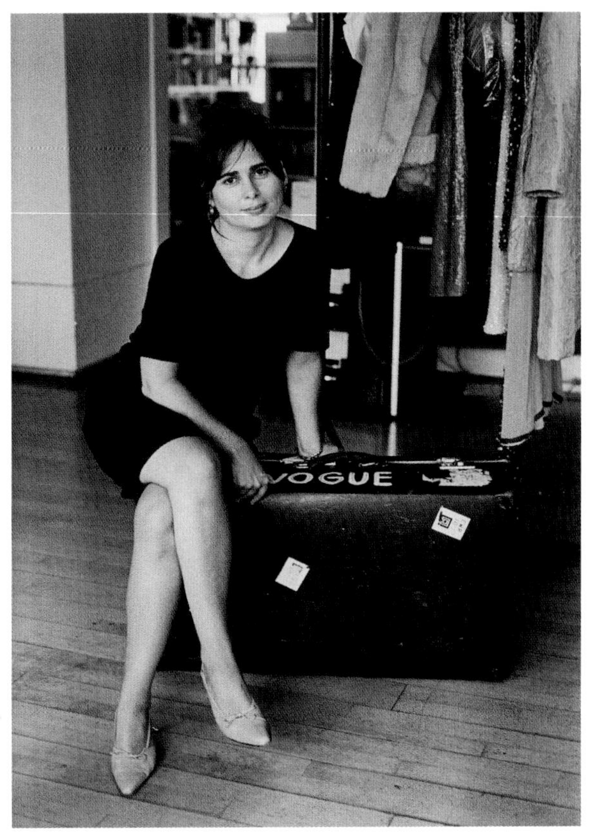
VOGUE

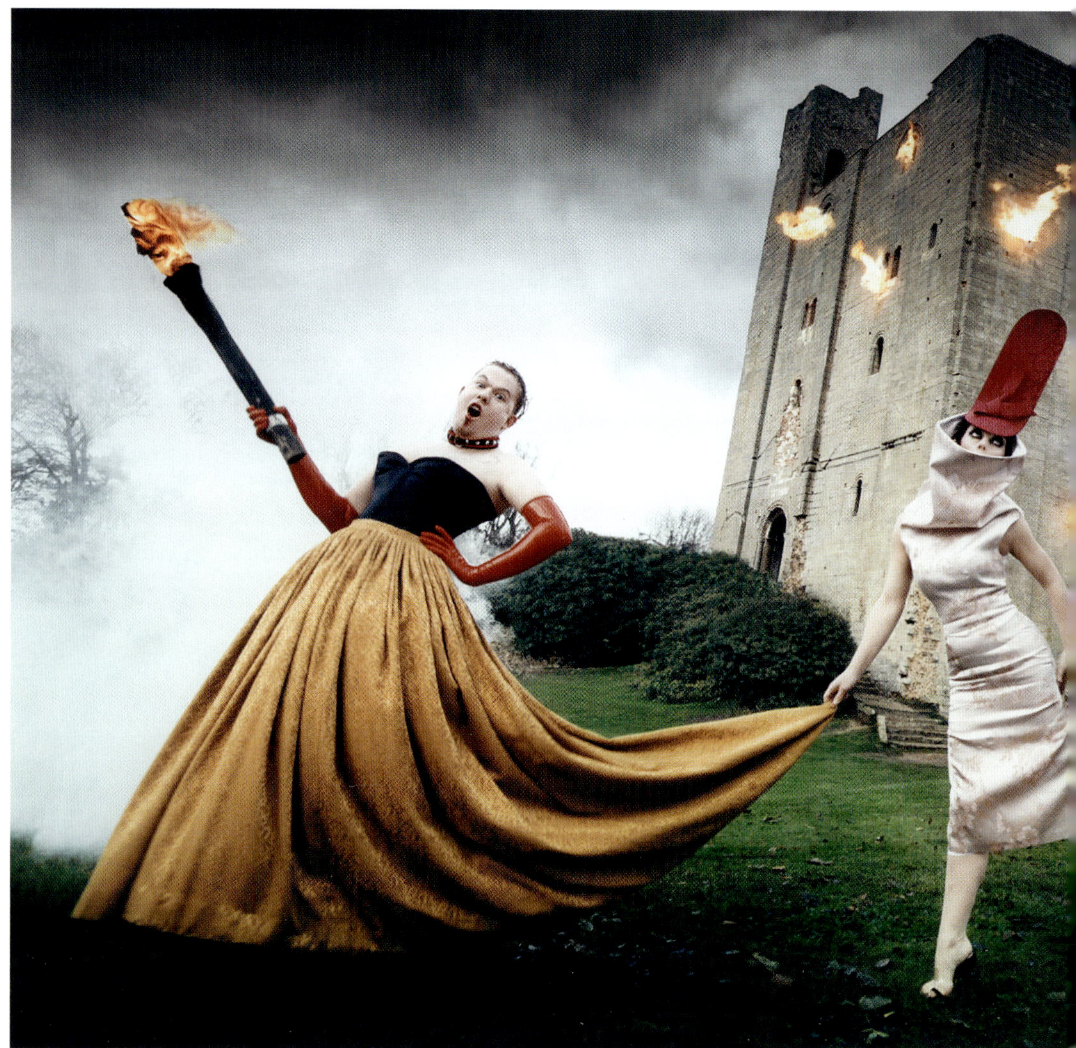

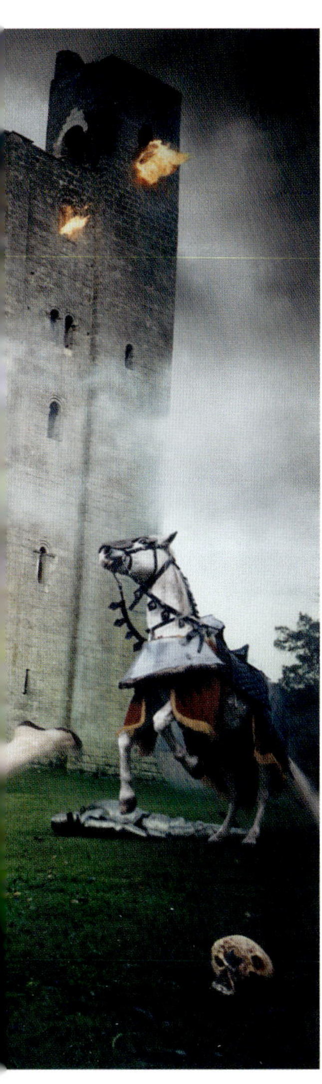

ALEXANDER MCQUEEN
(1969–2010) and ISABELLA BLOW
(1958–2007)
David LaChapelle, 1996
Chromogenic print, 734 x 1012mm
NPG P1403

This double portrait of Alexander McQueen
and Isabella Blow was published in the
March 1997 'Swinging London' edition
of *Vanity Fair*, under the title 'The
Provocateurs'. McQueen was a fashion
designer famed for his conceptually daring
approach. Blow, a fashion stylist, was
a great champion of McQueen, buying
his graduate collection 'Jack the Ripper
Stalks his Victims' in 1992. For this
photograph, taken at Hedingham Castle,
Essex, the pair dressed in clothes designed
by McQueen, while Blow's hat is by
milliner Philip Treacy. Photographer
David LaChapelle (b.1963), who began
his career at Andy Warhol's *Interview*
magazine, subverts gender norms
and notions of chivalry in this image.
This photograph also acts as a theatrical
record of the sitters' playful friendship.

JIMMY CHOO (b.1948)
Bronwyn Kidd, 1997
Gelatin silver print, 293 x 279mm
NPG x87336

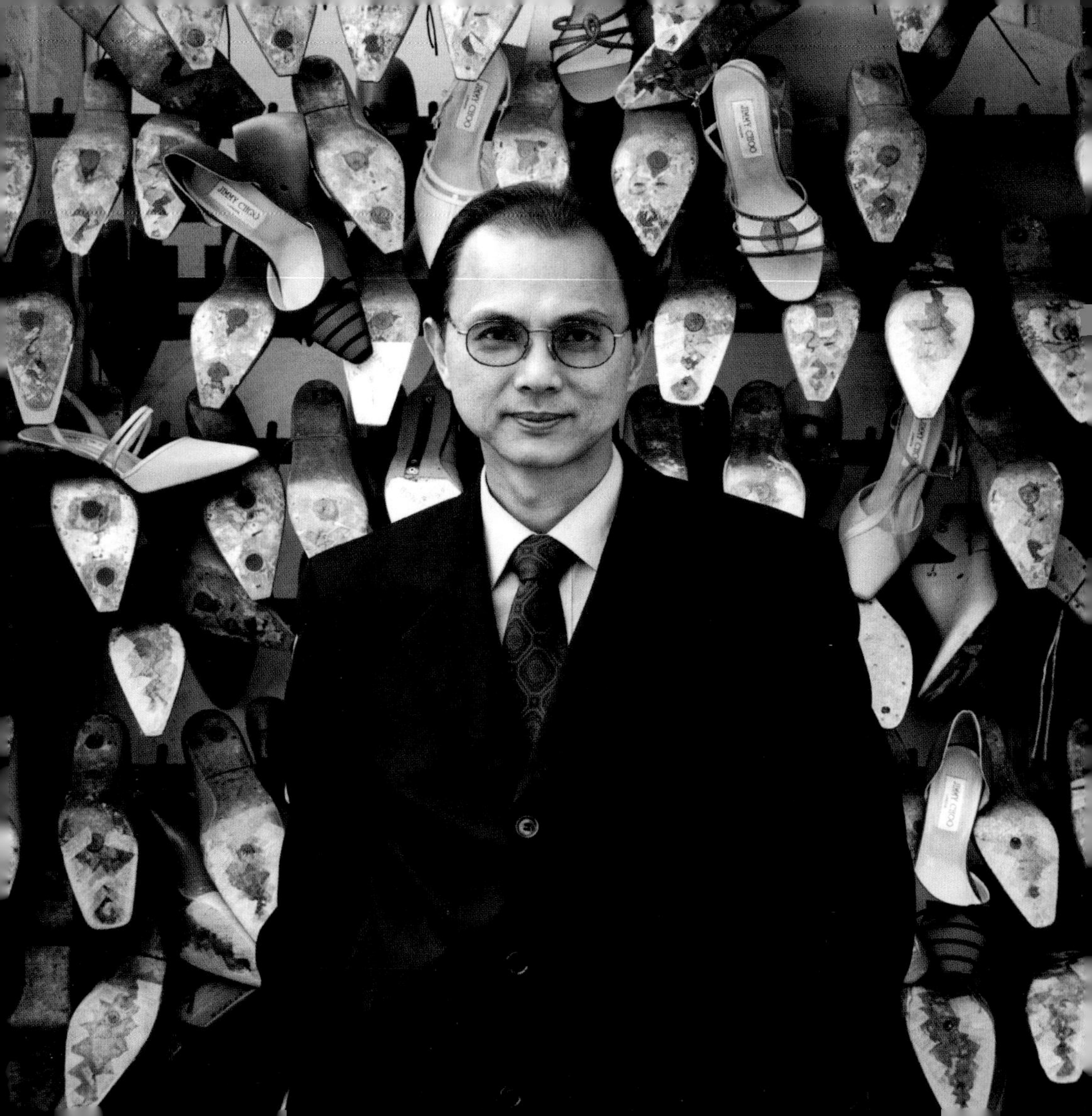

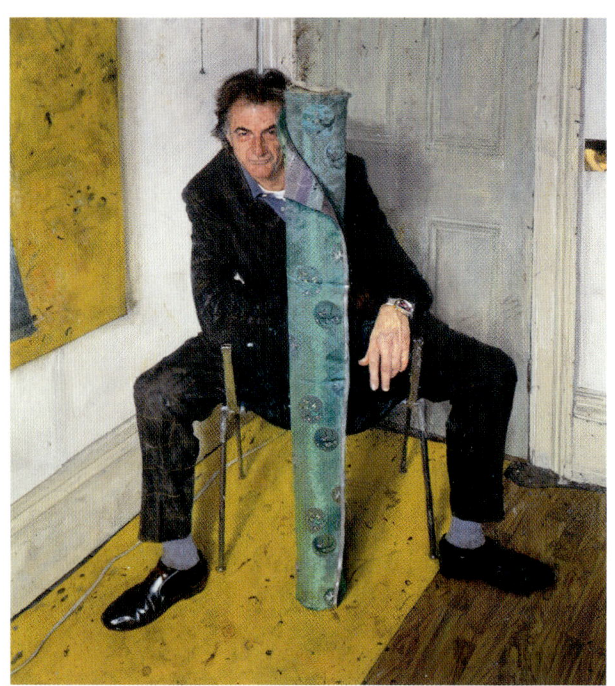

LEFT

SIR PAUL SMITH (b.1946)

James Lloyd, 1998

Oil on canvas, 1624 x 1451mm

NPG 6441

OPPOSITE

OZWALD BOATENG (b.1967)

Jillian Edelstein, 1997

Gelatin silver print, 305 x 245mm

NPG x87784

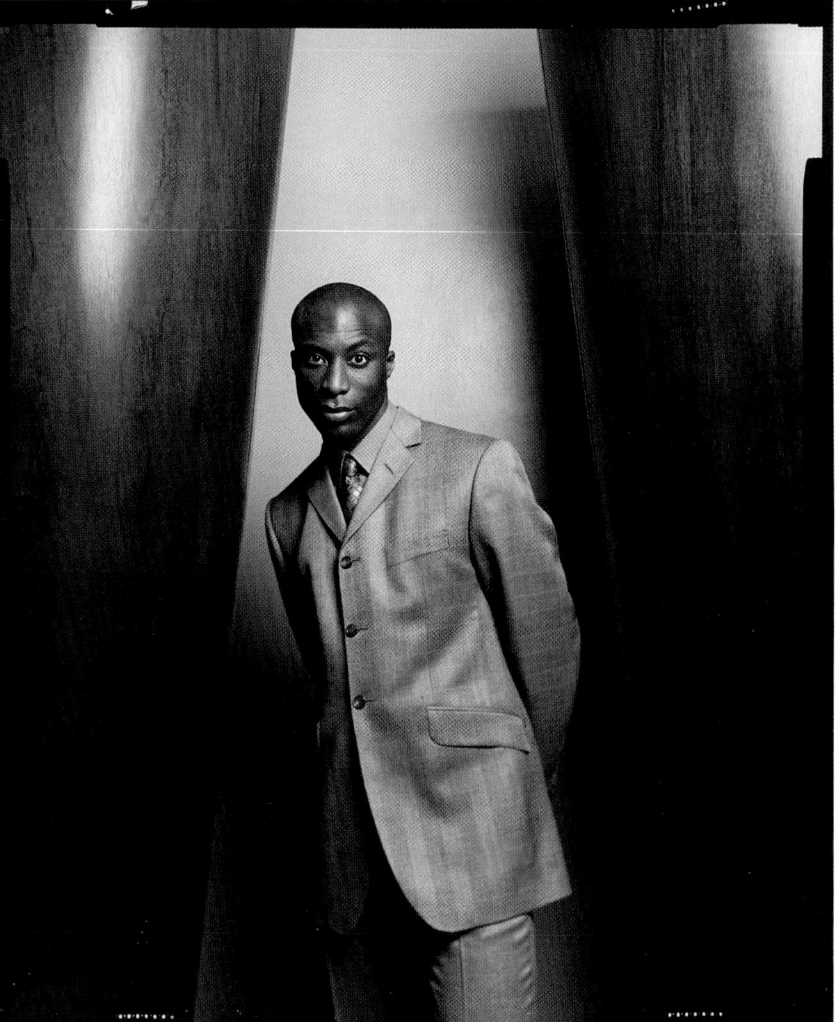

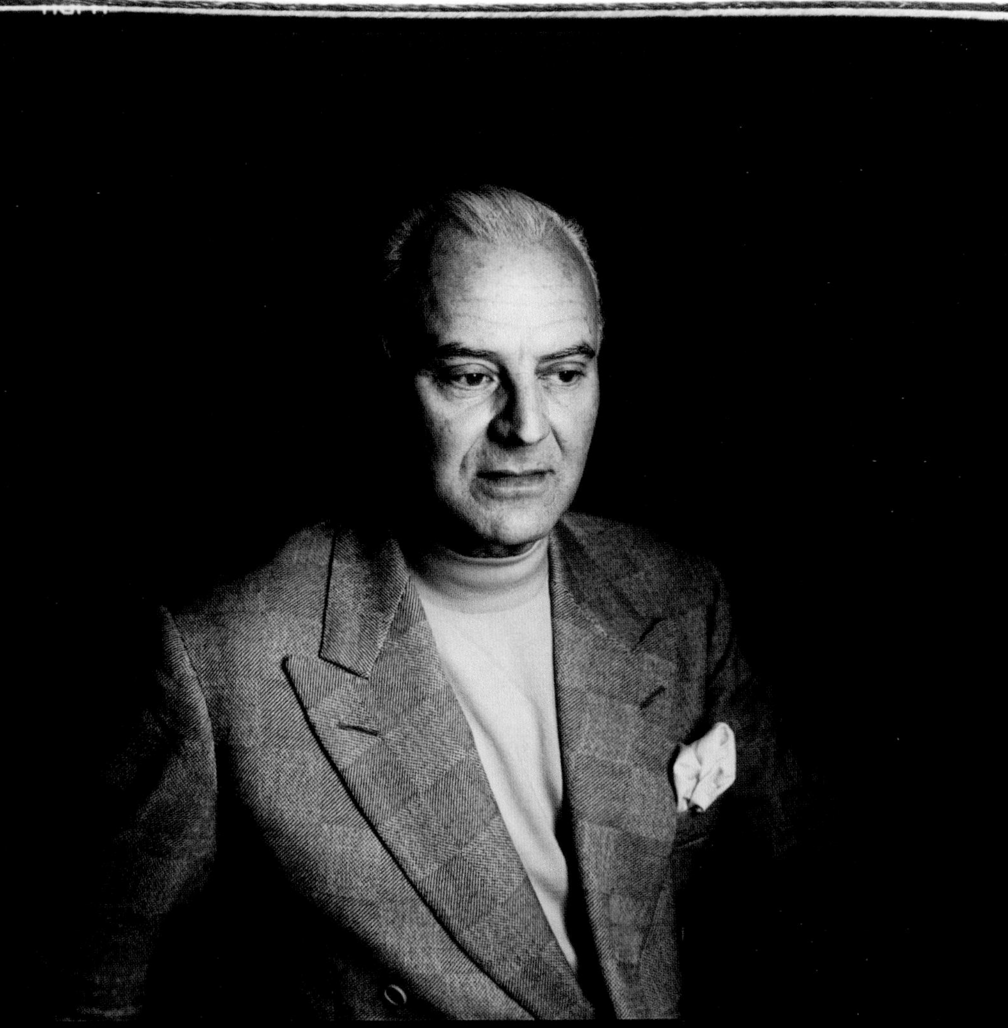

MANOLO BLAHNIK (b.1942)
Laurence Cendrowicz, 2002
Gelatin silver print, 350 x 343mm
NPG X126111

JOHN CHARLES GALLIANO

(b.1960)

Paolo Roversi, 2005

Inkjet print, 240 x 187mm

NPG P1278

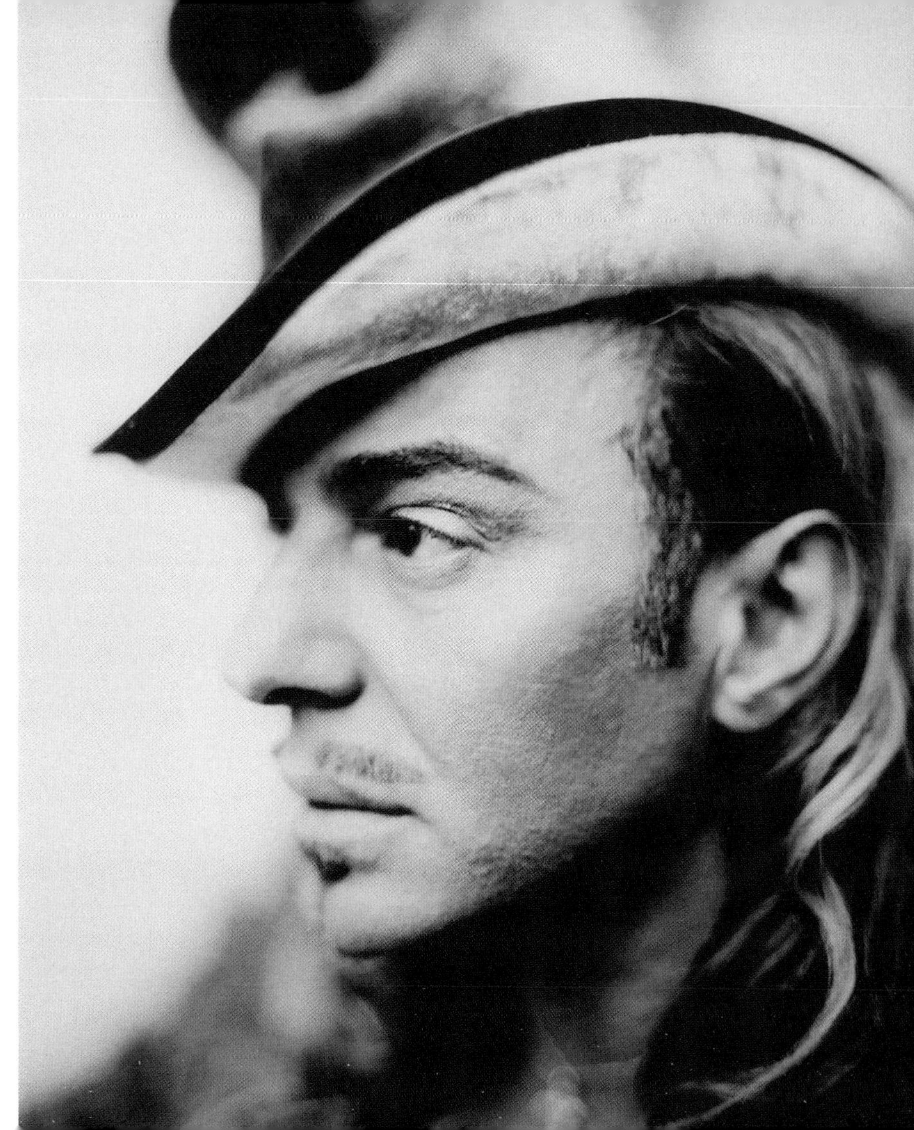

DAME ANNA WINTOUR (b.1949)

Alex Katz, 2009

Oil on linen, 1524 x 2134mm

NPG 6908

As editor-in-chief of American *Vogue* since 1988, British-born Dame Anna Wintour (b.1949) has made a significant contribution to the international fashion industry. Previously editor of British *Vogue* (1984–7), Wintour is credited with boosting the circulation and reinvigorating both titles. In 2013, Wintour became artistic director for Condé Nast, *Vogue*'s publisher. Based on studies from life, this painting was the first time Wintour sat for a portrait. Alex Katz (b.1927) has said: 'Painting Anna was like shooting a fish in a barrel. There was no way I could miss it.'

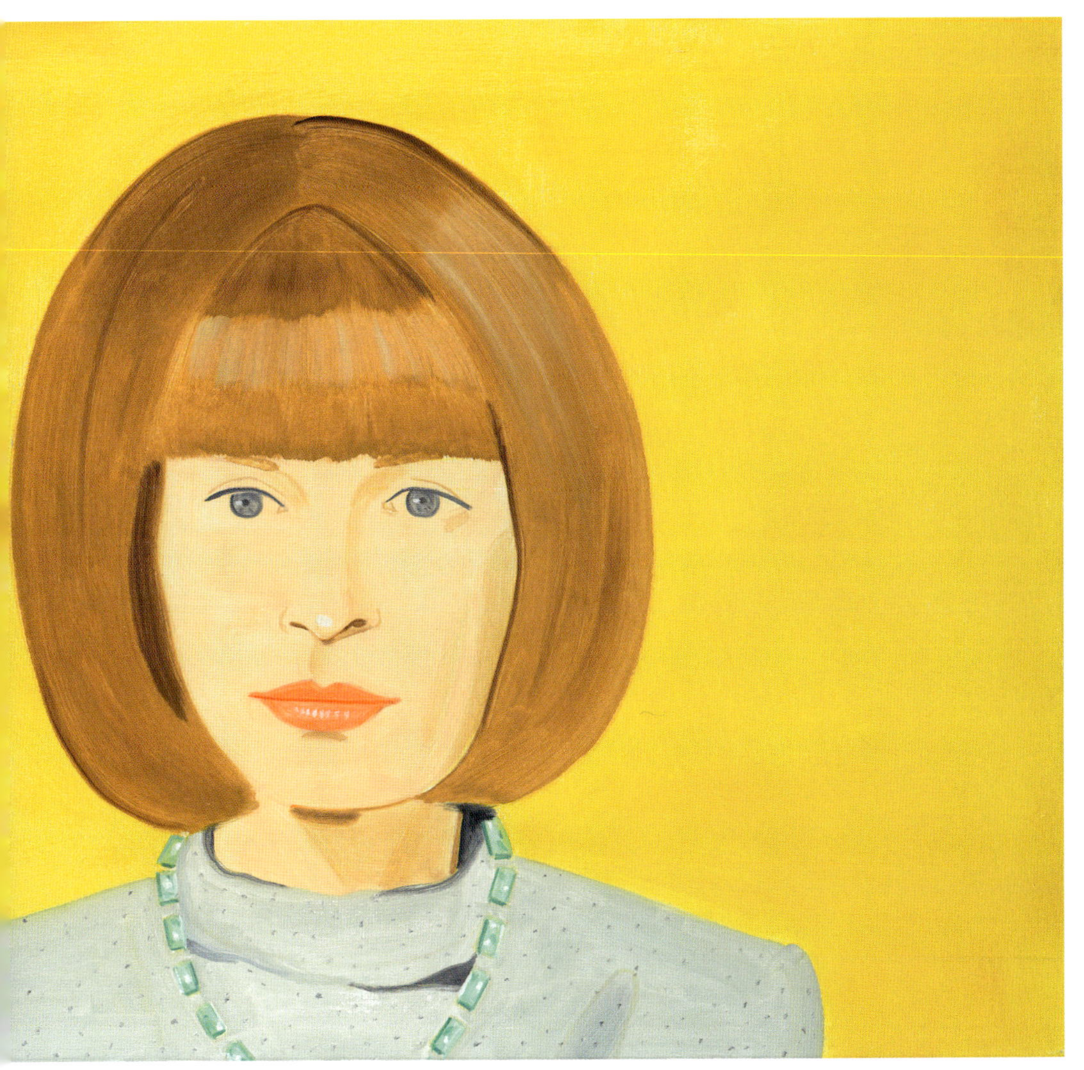

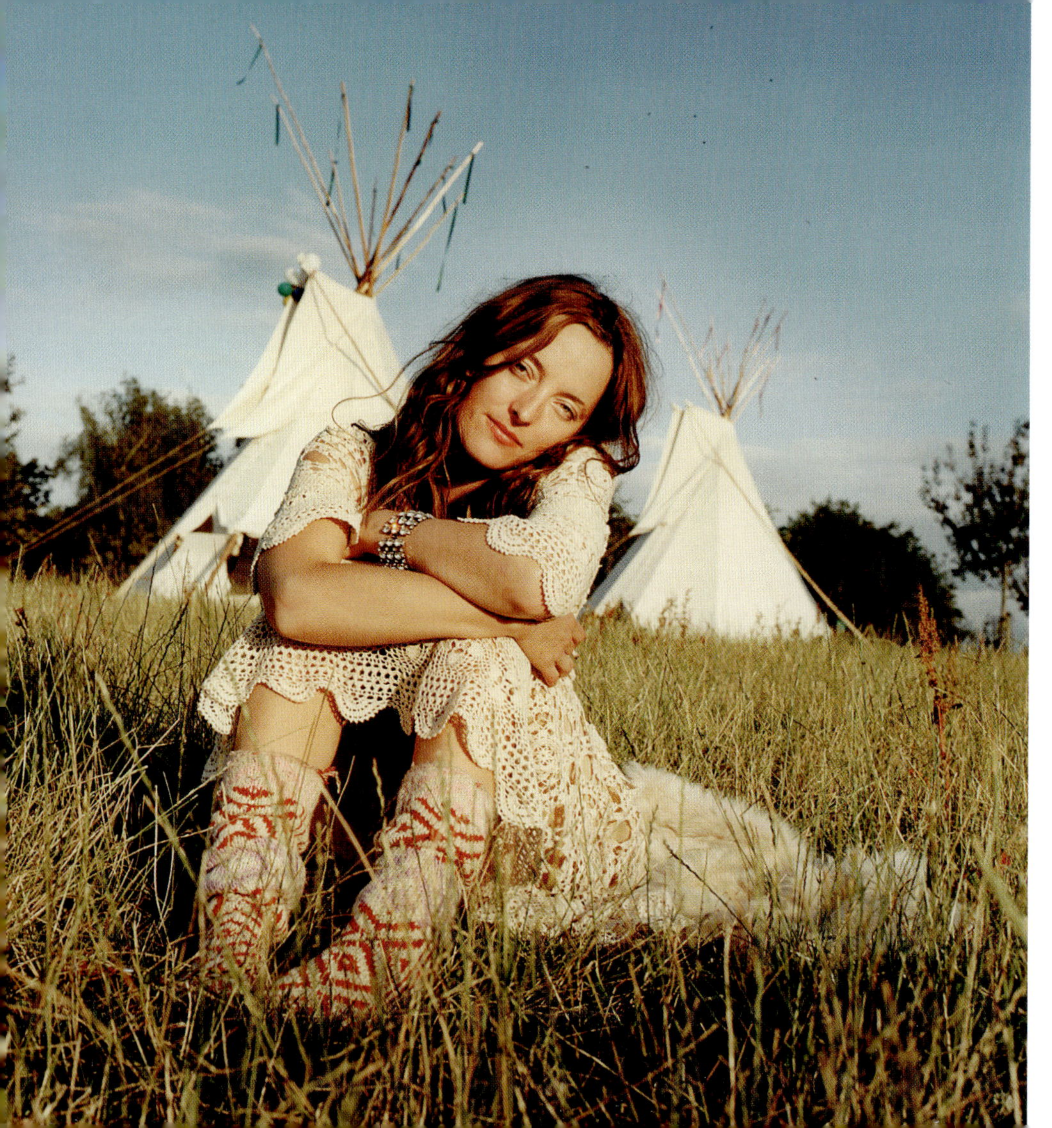

ALICE TEMPERLEY (b.1975)

Venetia Dearden, 2004

Chromogenic print, 405 x 357mm

NPG x127160

LUELLA BARTLEY (b.1974)

Ellen Nolan, 2001

Chromogenic print, 381 x 306mm

NPG x135702

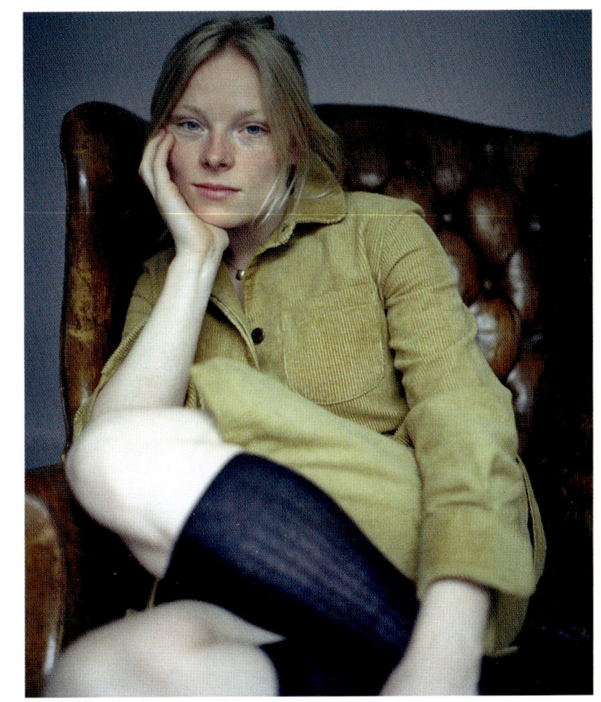

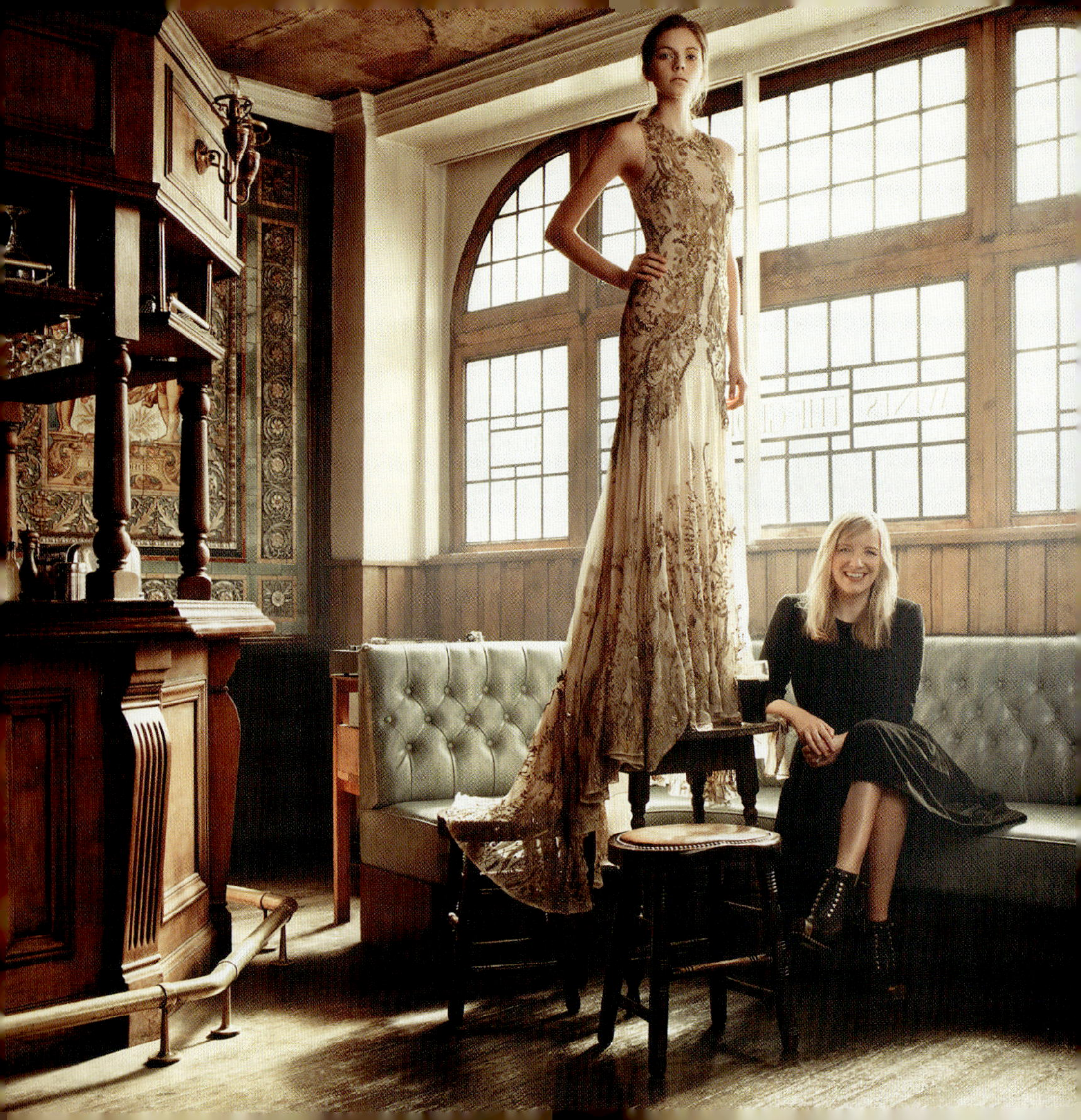

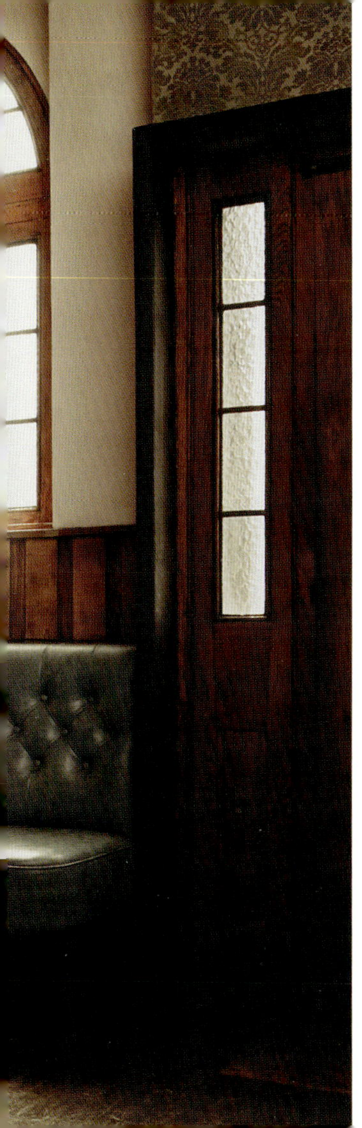

SARAH BURTON (b.1974)
and model
Jason Bell, 2011
Inkjet print, 278 x 363mm
NPG x199354

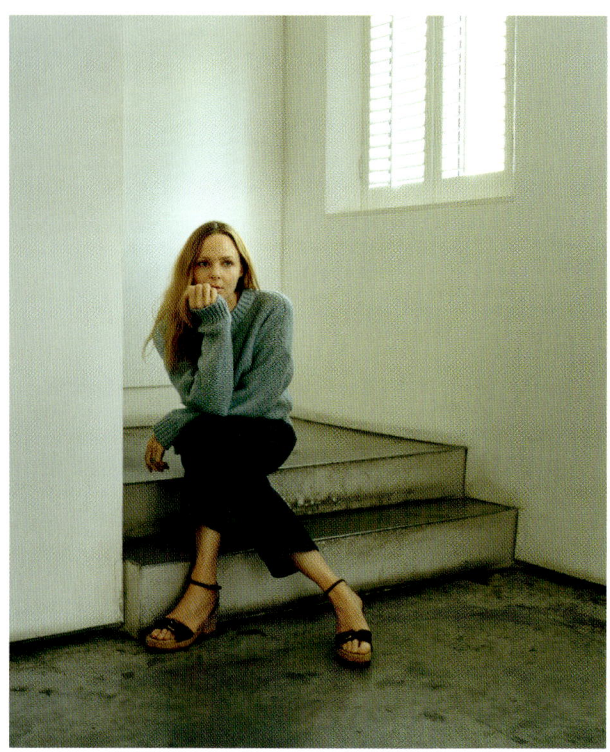

LEFT

STELLA MCCARTNEY (b.1972)

Emma Hardy, 2011

Chromogenic print, 634 x 508mm

NPG P1765

OPPOSITE

MARGARET HOWELL (b.1946)

David Vintiner, 2013

Chromogenic print, 464 x 367mm

NPG x139785

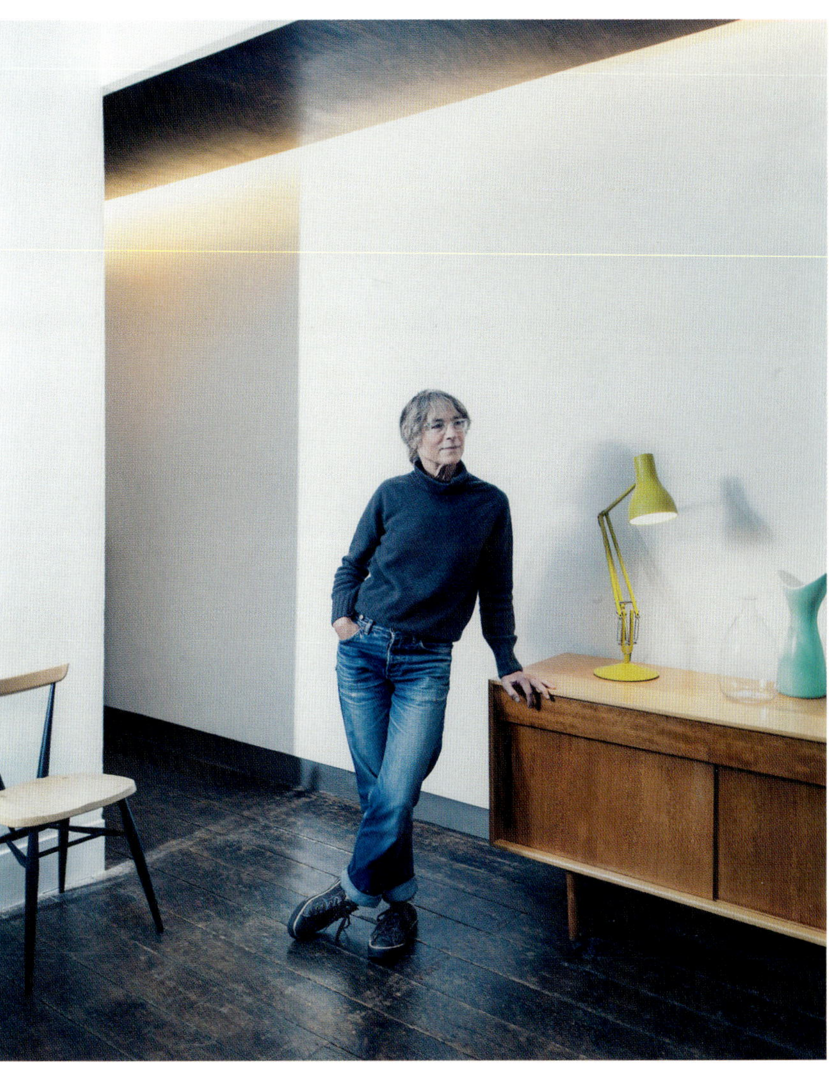

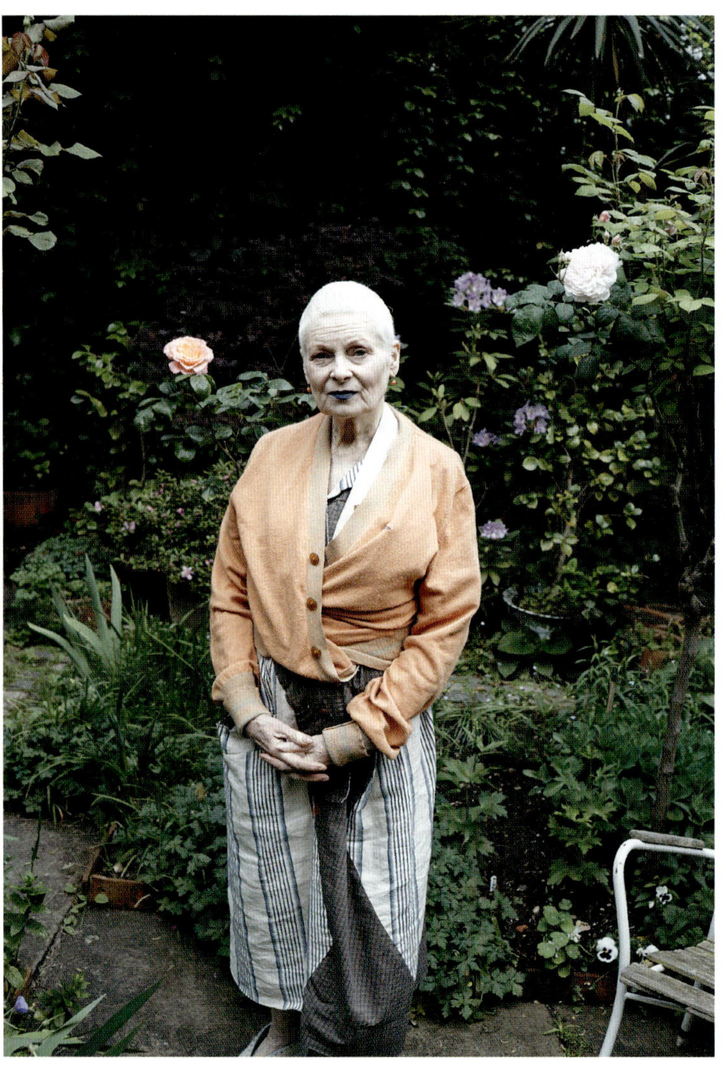

DAME VIVIENNE WESTWOOD
(b.1941) (*Vivienne In Her Garden, London 2014*)
Juergen Teller, 2014
Chromogenic print, 1219 x 812mm
NPG P1980

In the 1970s, Dame Vivienne Westwood co-founded the boutique Let It Rock on King's Road in London, later renamed SEX, which defined British punk. Twice named Designer of the Year (1990, 1991), she is also a campaigner for human rights, environmental issues and climate change. German-born Juergen Teller (b.1964) has shot Westwood's fashion campaigns since 2007. This informal and intimate portrait by her long-time collaborator shows Westwood in the garden of her London home.

EDWARD ENNINFUL (b.1972)
Simon Frederick, 2016
Inkjet print, 420 x 295mm
NPG P2042

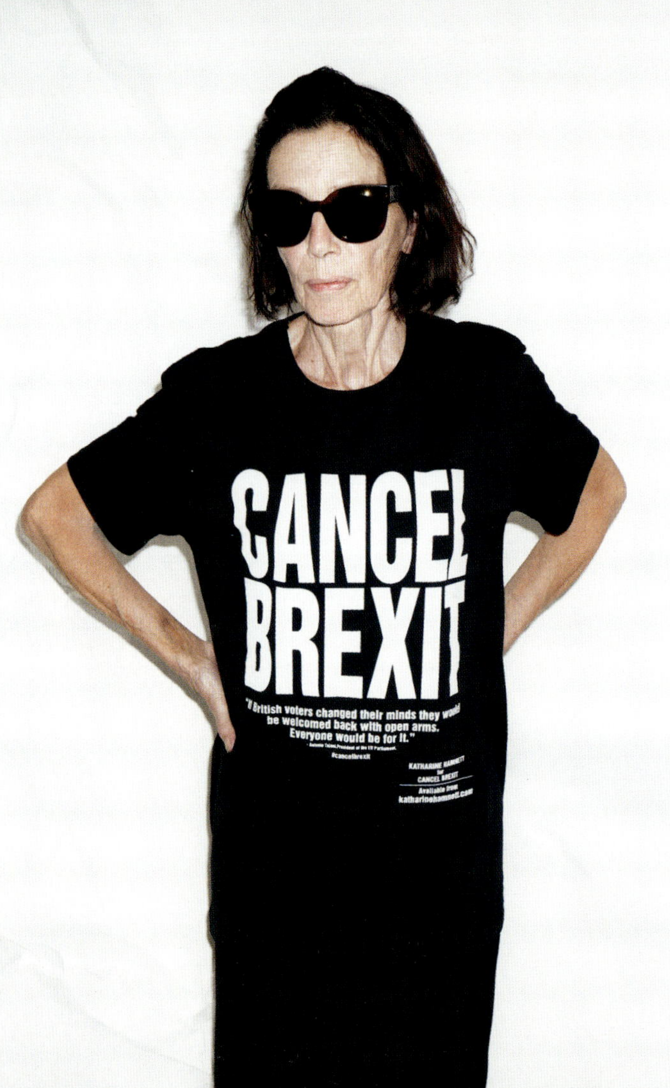

CANCEL
BREXIT
"If British voters changed their minds they would
be welcomed back with open arms.
Everyone would be for it."
- Antonio Tajani, President of the EU Parliament.
#cancelbrexit
KATHARINE HAMNETT
for
CANCEL BREXIT
Available from
katharinehamnett.com

KATHARINE HAMNETT (b.1947)
Ben McMahon, 2017
Inkjet print, 460 x 355mm
NPG x200140

THELMA GOLDEN (b.1965)
and DURO OLOWU (b.1965)
(*Thelma & Duro*)
Catherine Opie, 2017
Inkjet print, 1956 x 1473mm
NPG P2076

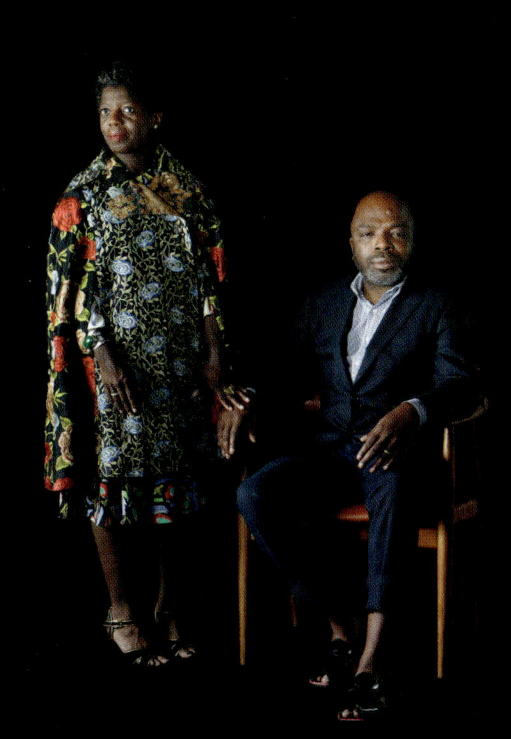

ILLUSTRATED FASHION

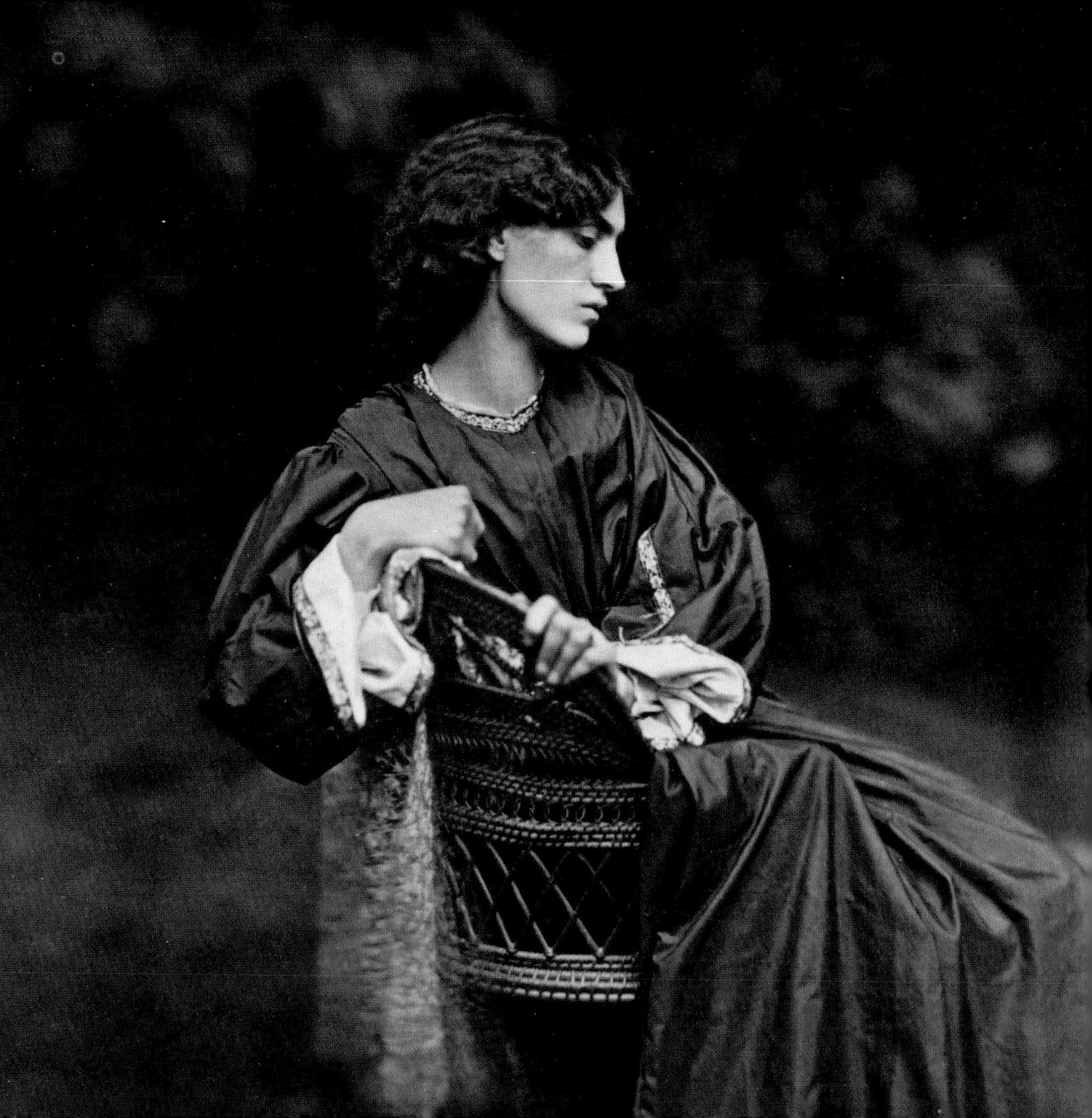

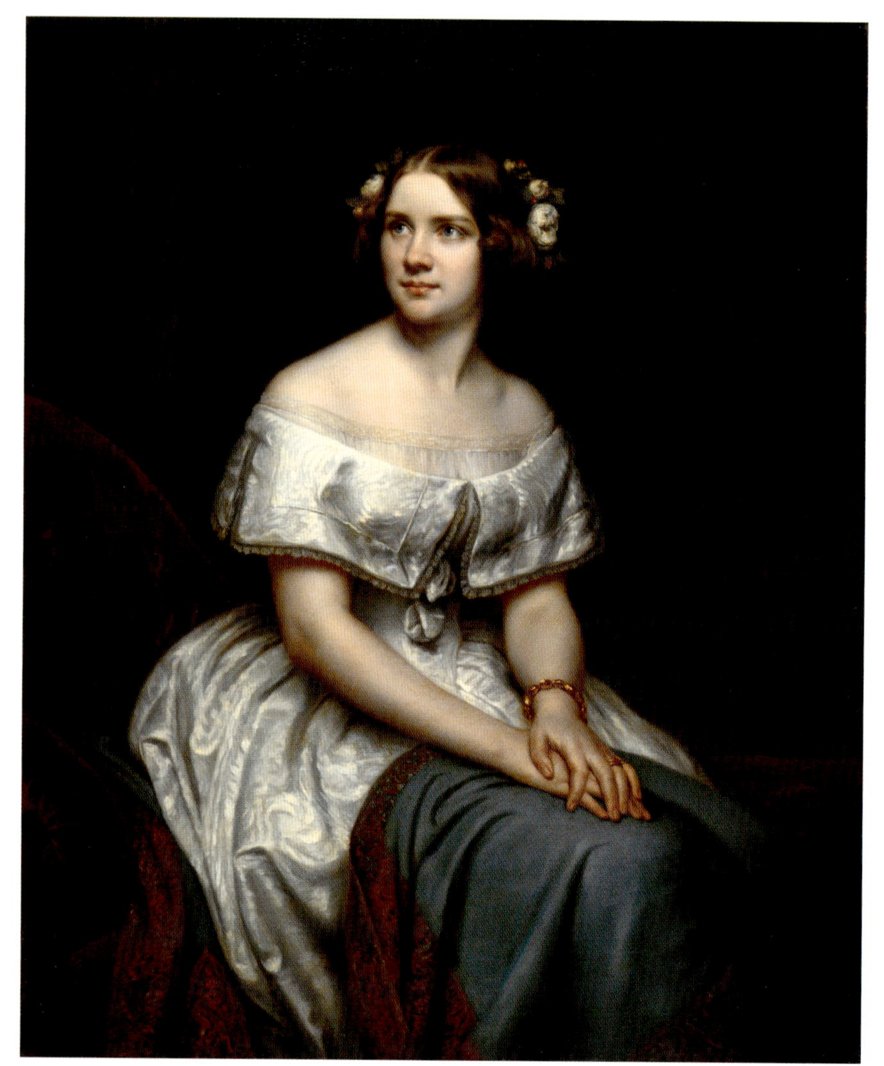

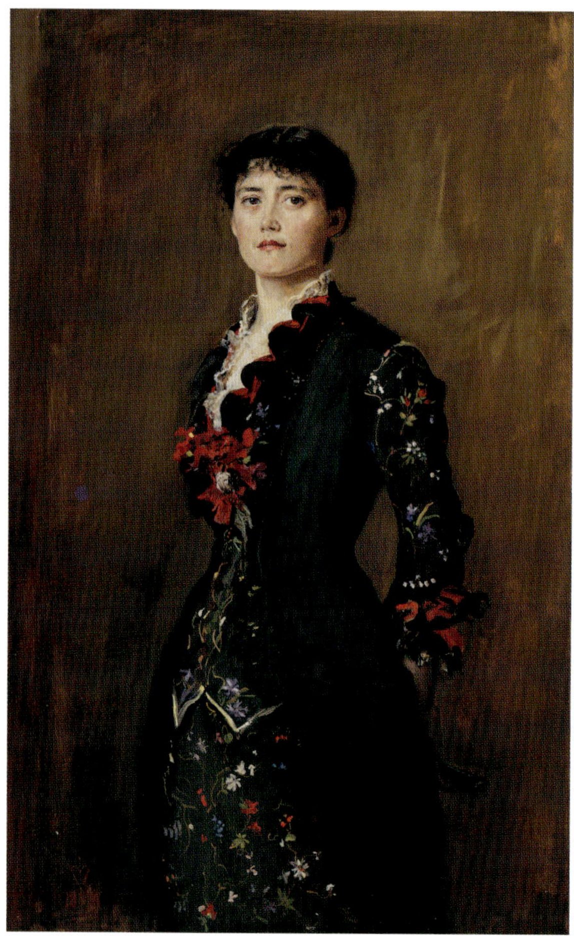

LEFT
LOUISE JANE JOPLING
(1843–1933)
Sir John Everett Millais, 1st Bt, 1879
Oil on canvas, 1240 x 765mm
NPG 6612

OPPOSITE
ADELINA PATTI (1843–1919)
James Sant, exhibited 1886
Oil on canvas, 1099 x 851mm
NPG 3625

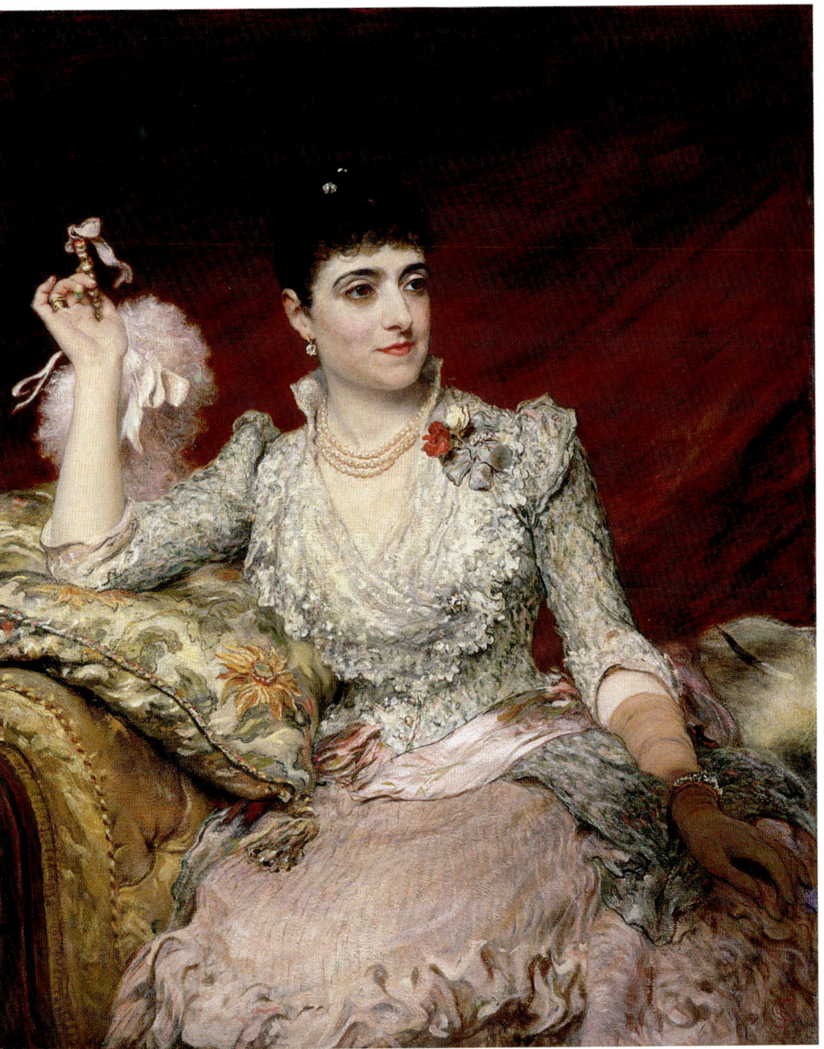

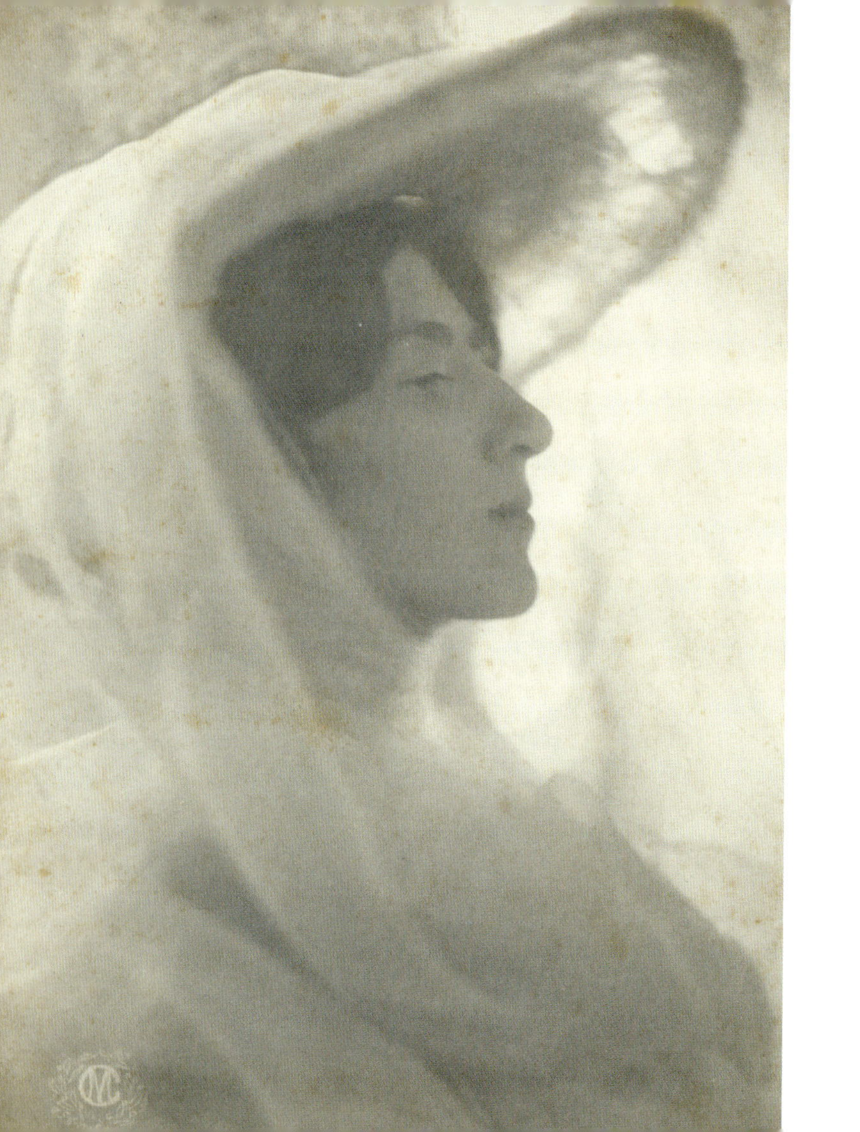

LADY OTTOLINE MORRELL

(1873–1938)

Cavendish Morton, c.1904

Platinum print, 156 x 109mm

NPG P479

Society hostess and patron of the arts, Lady Ottoline Morrell was known for her flair for fashion and idiosyncratic style. She entertained celebrated artists, writers and political figures at her home at 44 Bedford Square in Bloomsbury, London, and continued to do so at her subsequent residences, Garsington Manor in Oxfordshire and in Bloomsbury again at 10 Gower Street. In this pictorialist-inspired photograph, Cavendish Morton (1874–1939) portrays Morrell wrapped in delicate and soft fabric, crafting an image that creates an effect as if it has been softly painted.

KEIR HARDIE (1856–1915)

Arthur Clegg Weston, c.1892

Gelatin silver cabinet card, 166 x 108mm (detail)

NPG x13173

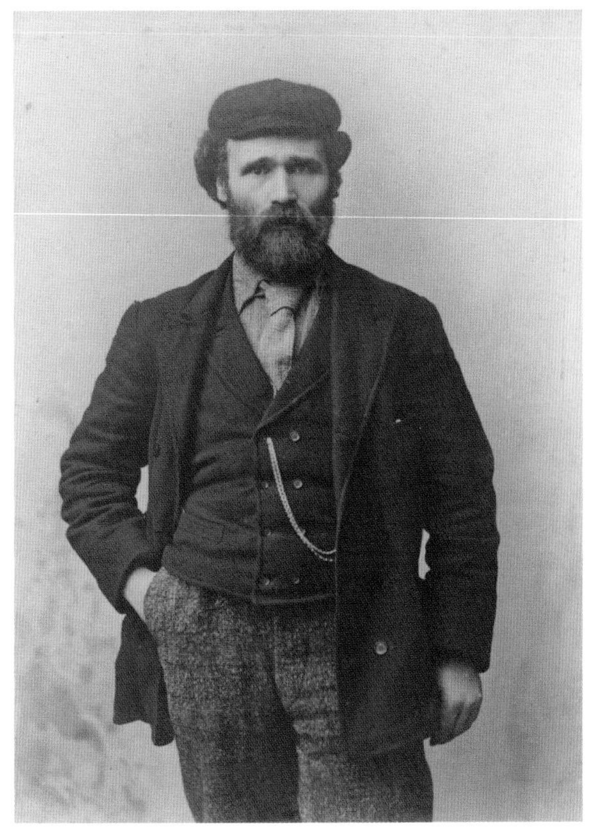

FANNY CORNFORTH

(1835– *c*.1909) (*Lady Lilith*)

Published in 1908 by The Medici Society Ltd

after Dante Gabriel Rossetti work of 1867

Chromolithograph, 662 x 482mm

NPG D37339

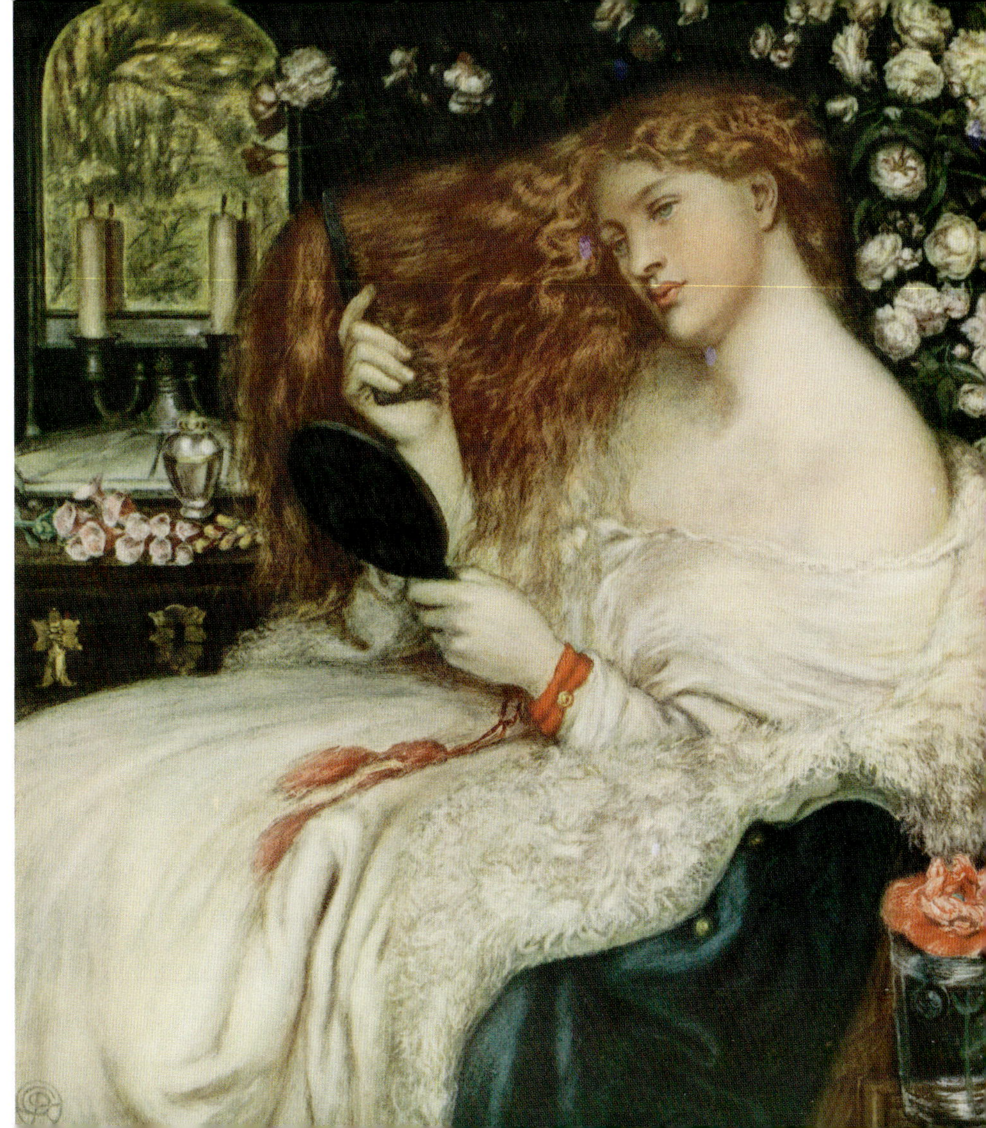

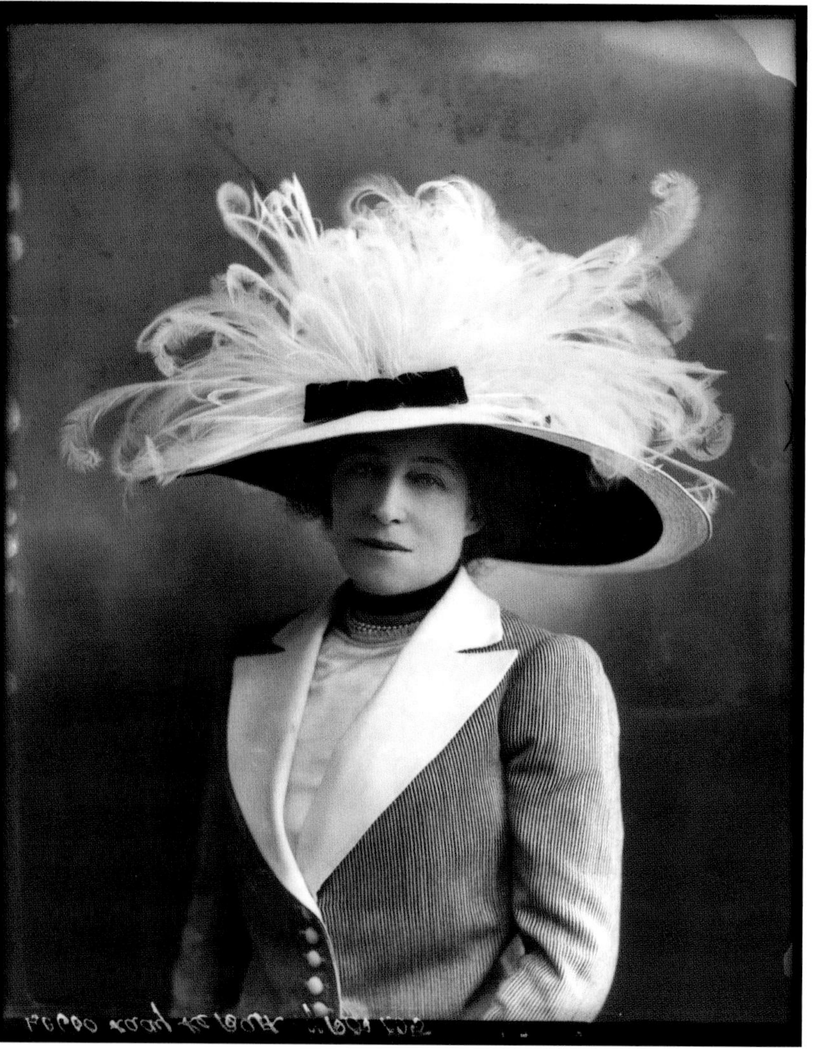

OPPOSITE

LILLIE LANGTRY (1853–1929)

Bassano Ltd, 1911

Whole-plate glass negative

NPG x127699

RIGHT

MADAME JUNE (dates unknown)

Bassano Ltd, 1919

Whole-plate glass negative

NPG x33783

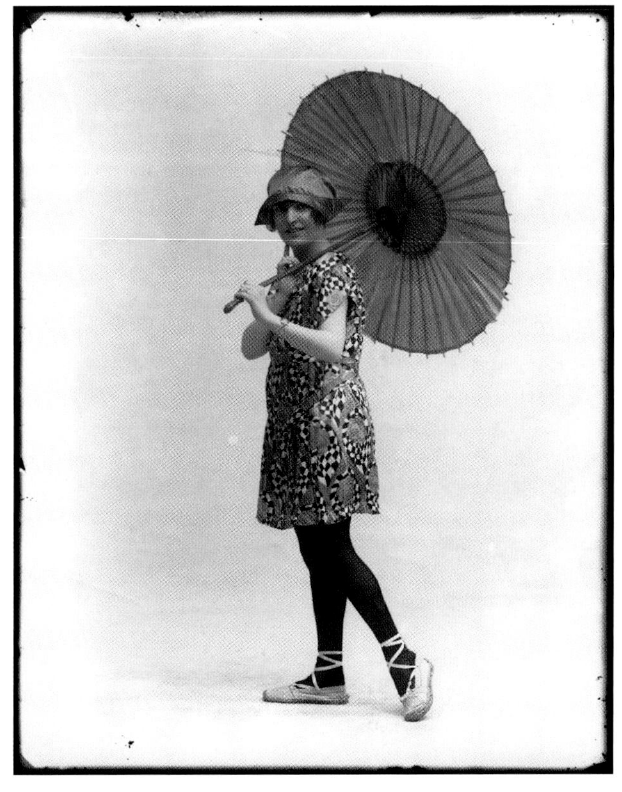

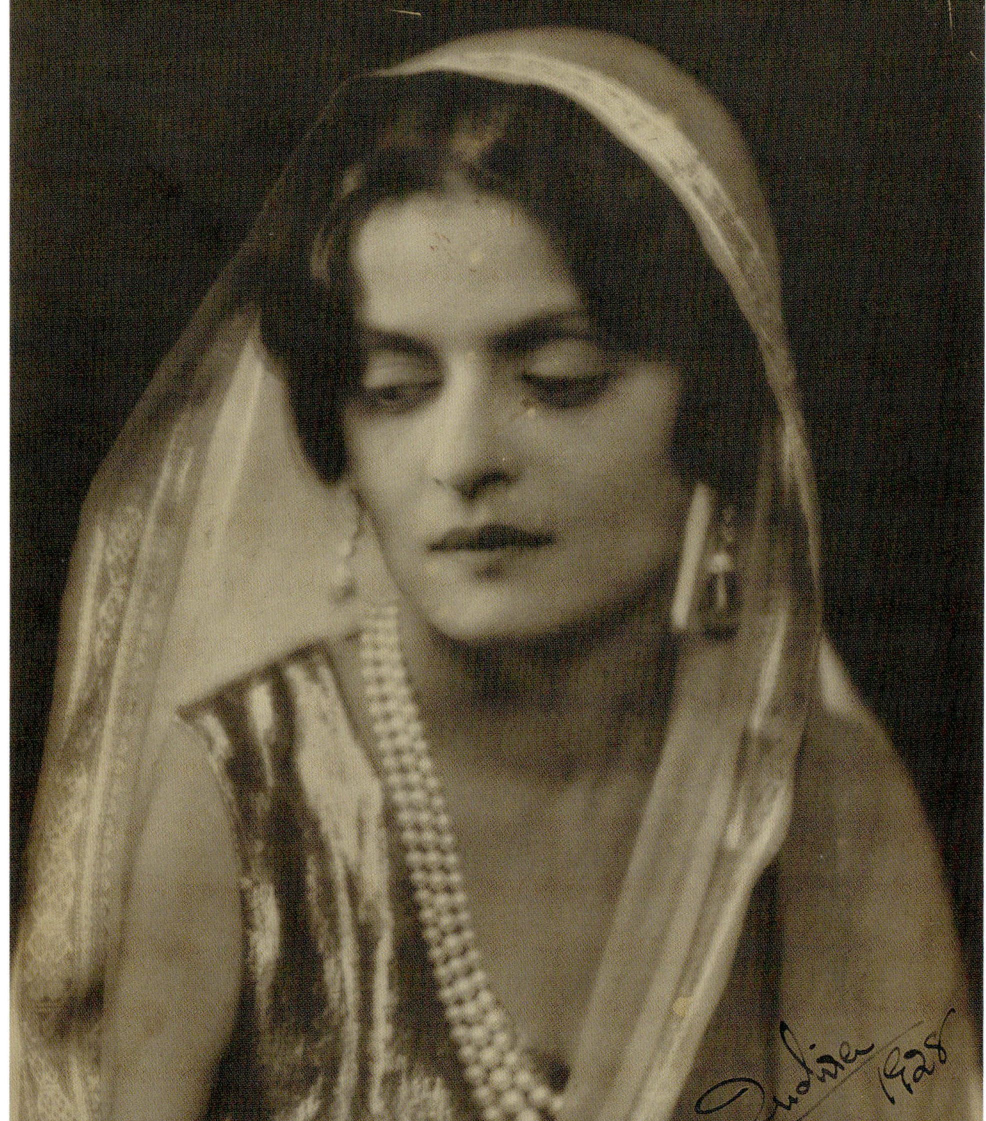
1928

INDIRA DEVI, MAHARANI
OF COOCH BEHAR (1892–1968)
Dorothy Wilding, 1928
Chlorobromide print, 280 x 225mm
NPG x6366

DORIS ZINKEISEN (1897–1991)

Self-portrait, exhibited 1929

Oil on canvas, 1072 x 866mm

NPG 6487

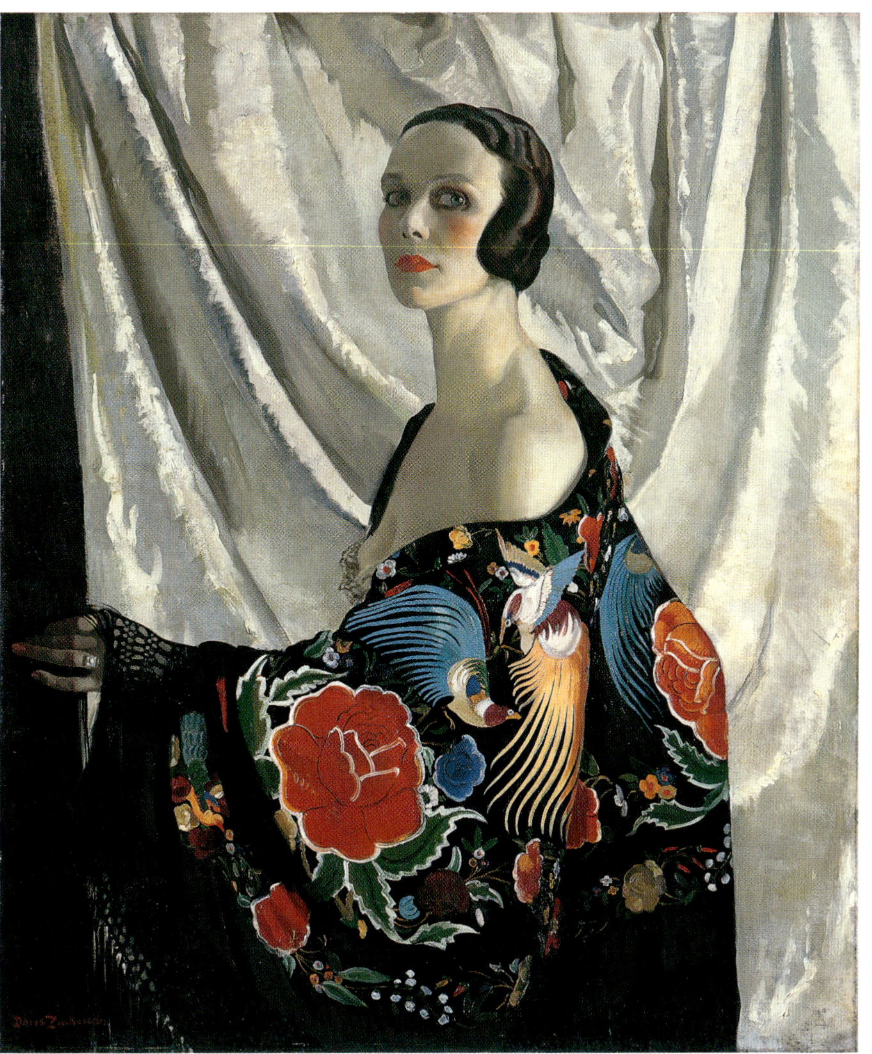

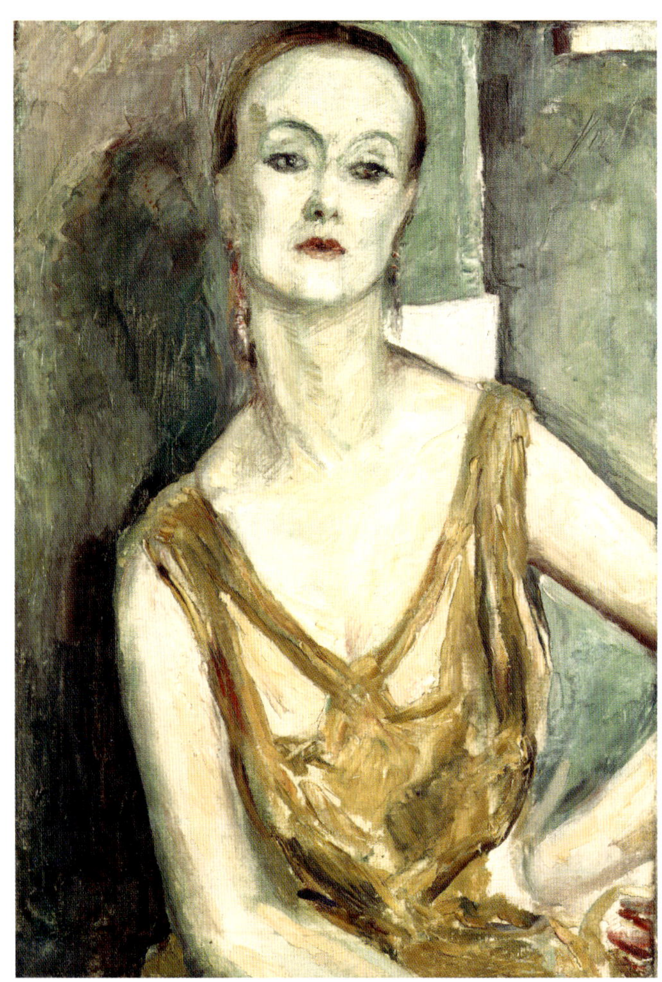

HARRIET COHEN (1895–1967)
Ronald Ossory Dunlop, c.1930
Oil on canvas, 760 x 507mm
NPG 6165

Harriet Cohen was a well-known pianist.
Although particularly associated with
J.S. Bach's music, Cohen performed a
wide repertoire of classic as well as
contemporary music. Constant Lambert,
among others, wrote for her, and Sir
Arnold Bax, a close friend, composed
*Concertante for Orchestra with Pianoforte
Solo (Left Hand)* for her after she lost
the use of her right hand in 1948. In this
painting by Ronald Ossory Dunlop
(1894–1973), Cohen wears a low-neck and
sleeveless dress – the kind of evening
attire that she wore when giving recitals.
Her hair is tied back in a bun or chignon
fashionable at the time.

JOAN MAUDE (1908–98)
Madame Yevonde, 1932
Vivex colour print, 356 x 278mm
NPG x26032

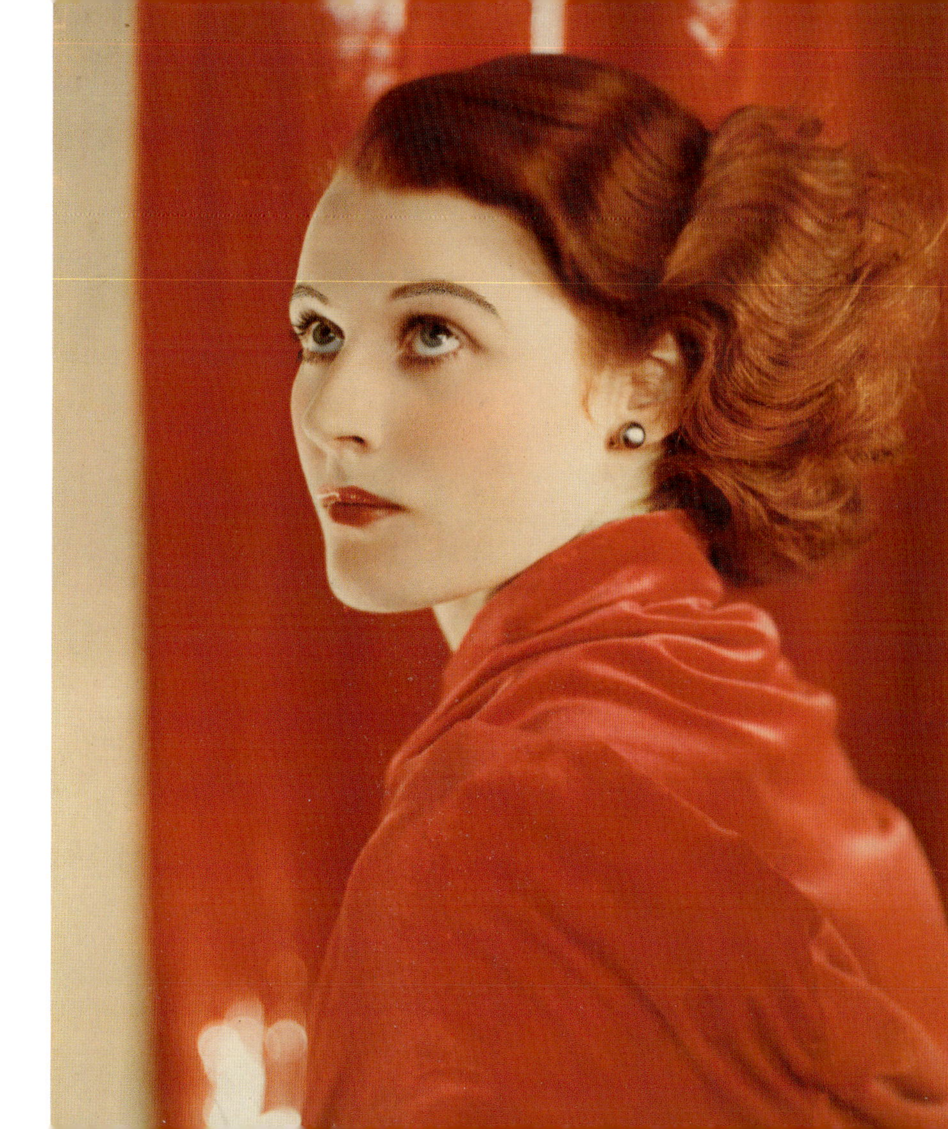

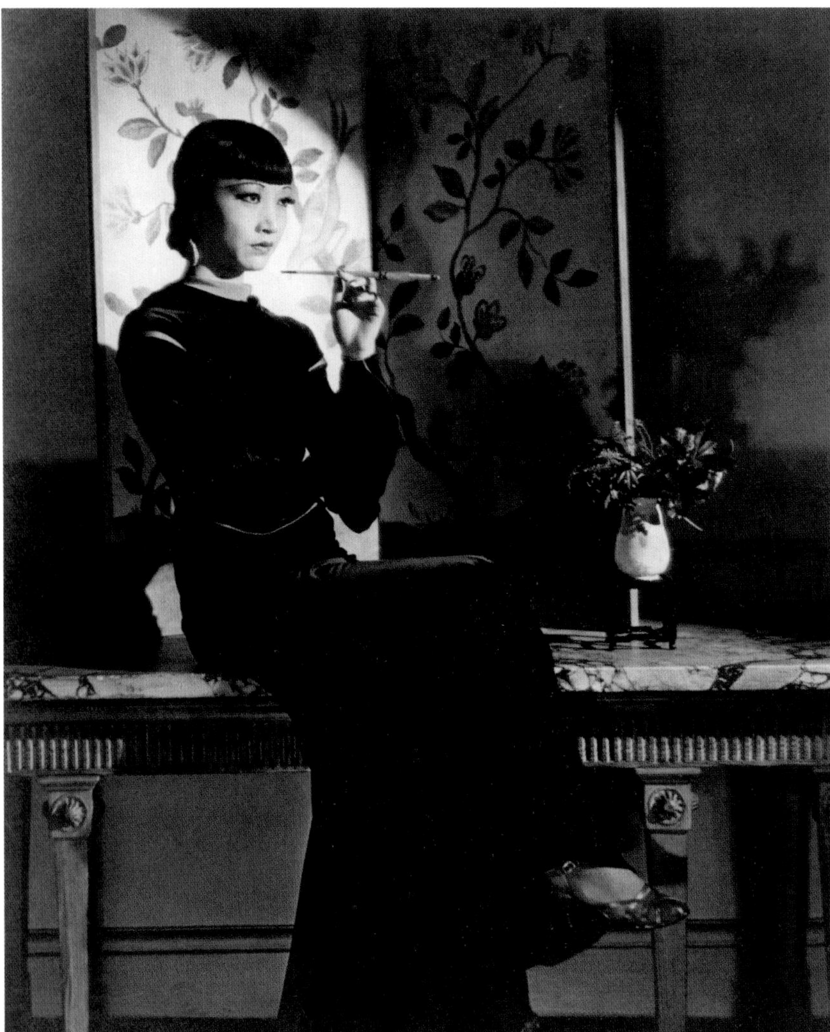

OPPOSITE

ANNA MAY WONG (1905–61)

Francis Goodman, 1933

Half-plate film negative

NPG x68812

RIGHT

PRINCESS NATALIA PALEY

(1905–81)

Dorothy Wilding, 1934

Whole-plate film negative

NPG x35442

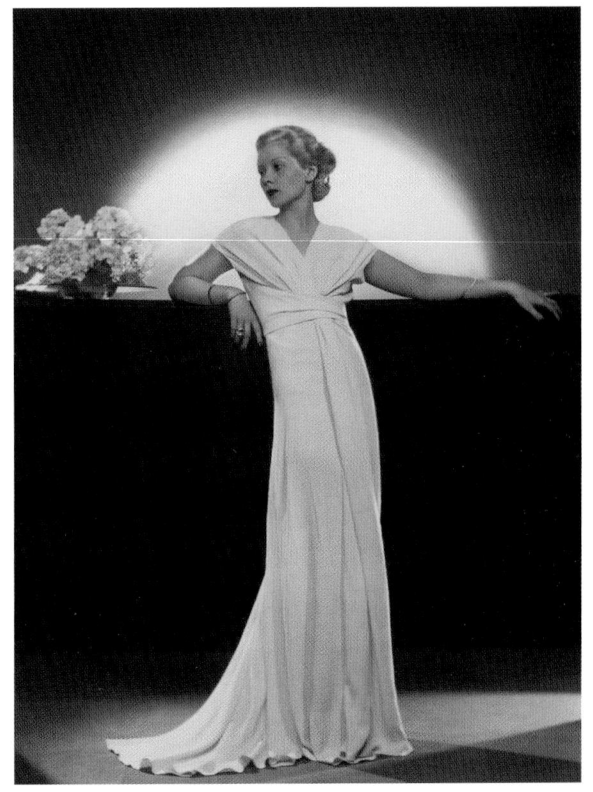

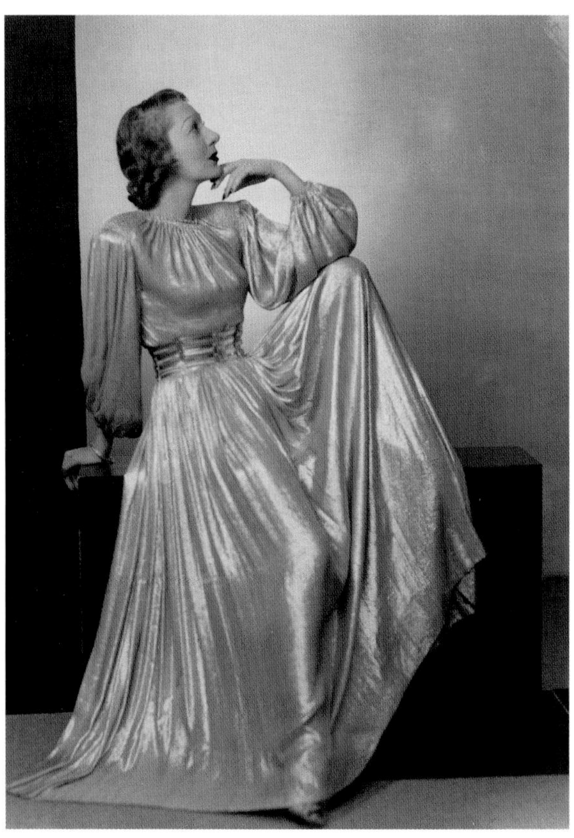

GERTRUDE LAWRENCE
(1898–1952)
Dorothy Wilding, 1939
Whole-plate film negative
NPG x29453

OPPOSITE

ELISABETH WELCH (1904–2003)
Unknown photographer, 1935
Gelatin silver print, 288 x 208mm
NPG x131704

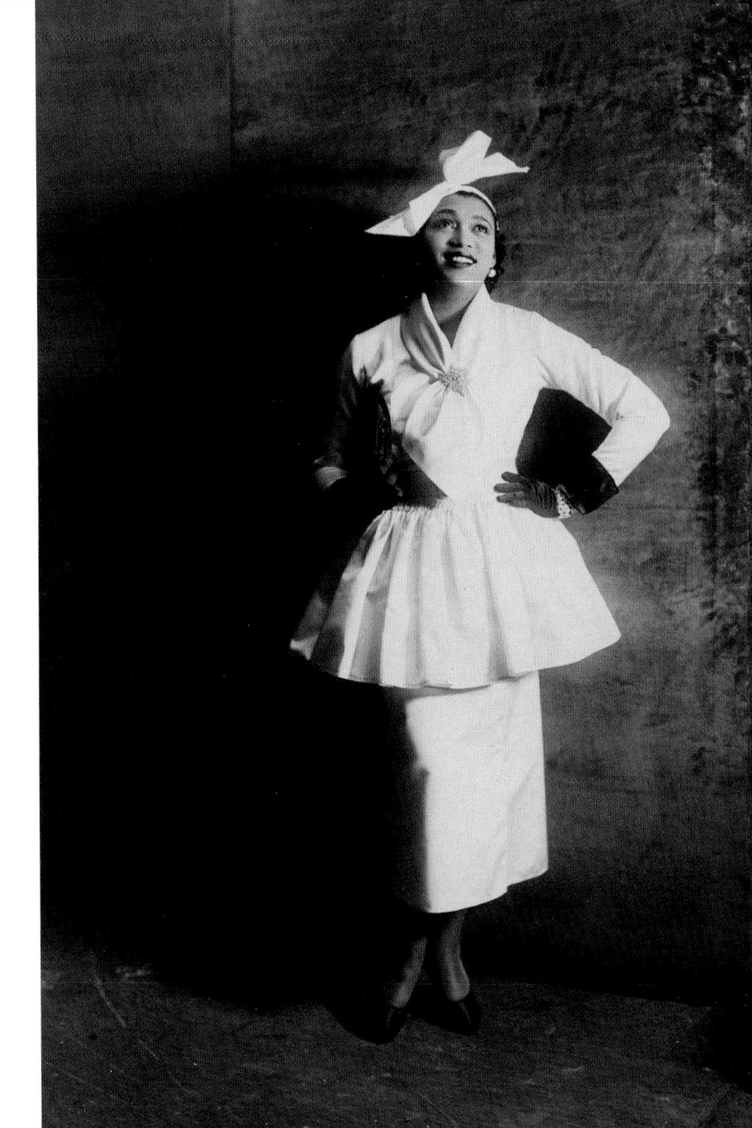

DIANA WYNYARD (1906–64)

Dorothy Wilding, 1937

Chlorobromide print, 433 x 333mm

NPG P870(16)

Diana Wynyard, one of a number of
British actresses whose successful careers
took them to Hollywood in the 1930s,
wears an evening dress based on the
classical Greek chiton, pinned at the
shoulders and belted at the waist in this
photograph. The classical influence is also
apparent in the studio setting, in which
photographer Dorothy Wilding (1893–1976)
posed the statuesque Wynyard resting
on a column. The neoclassical, modernist
styling and theatrical glamour that
characterise this photograph of Wynyard
are typical of Wilding's portraiture.

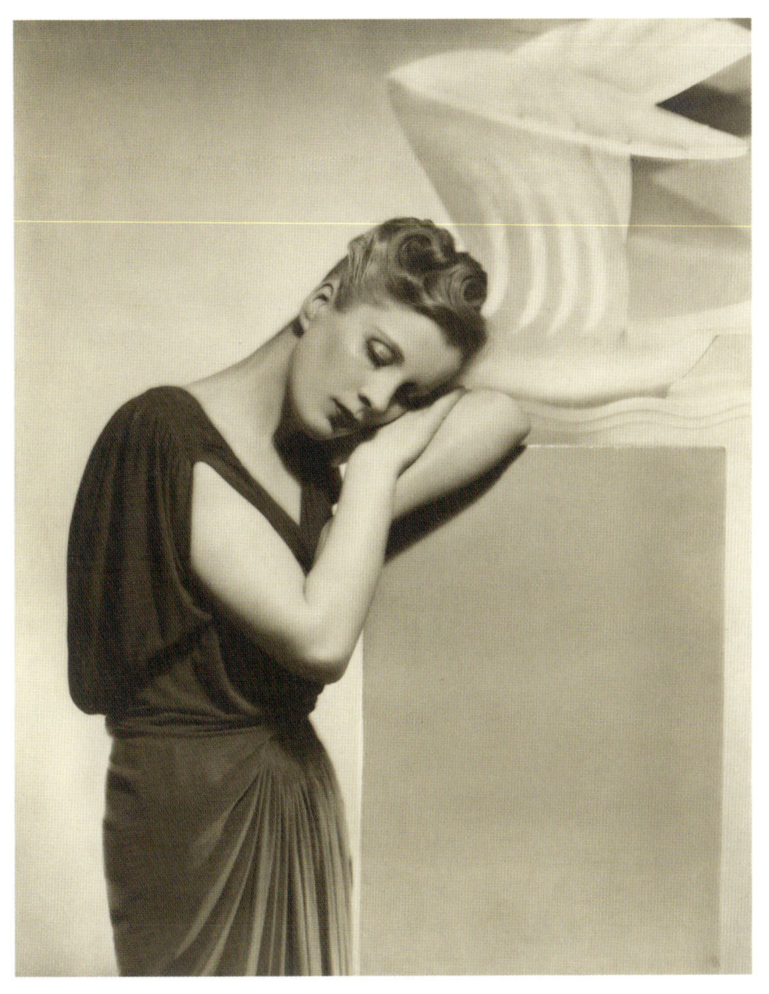

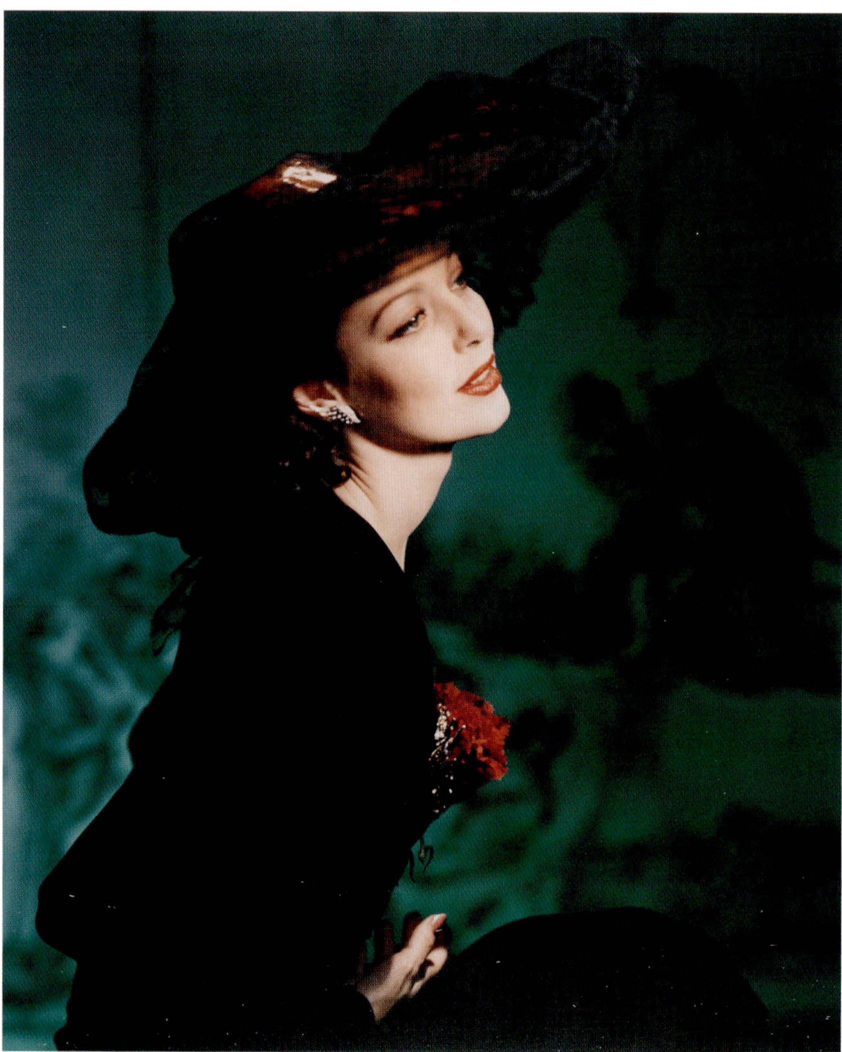

LORETTA YOUNG (1913–2000)
Horst P. Horst, 1941
Modern chromogenic print,
493 x 392mm
NPG x137763

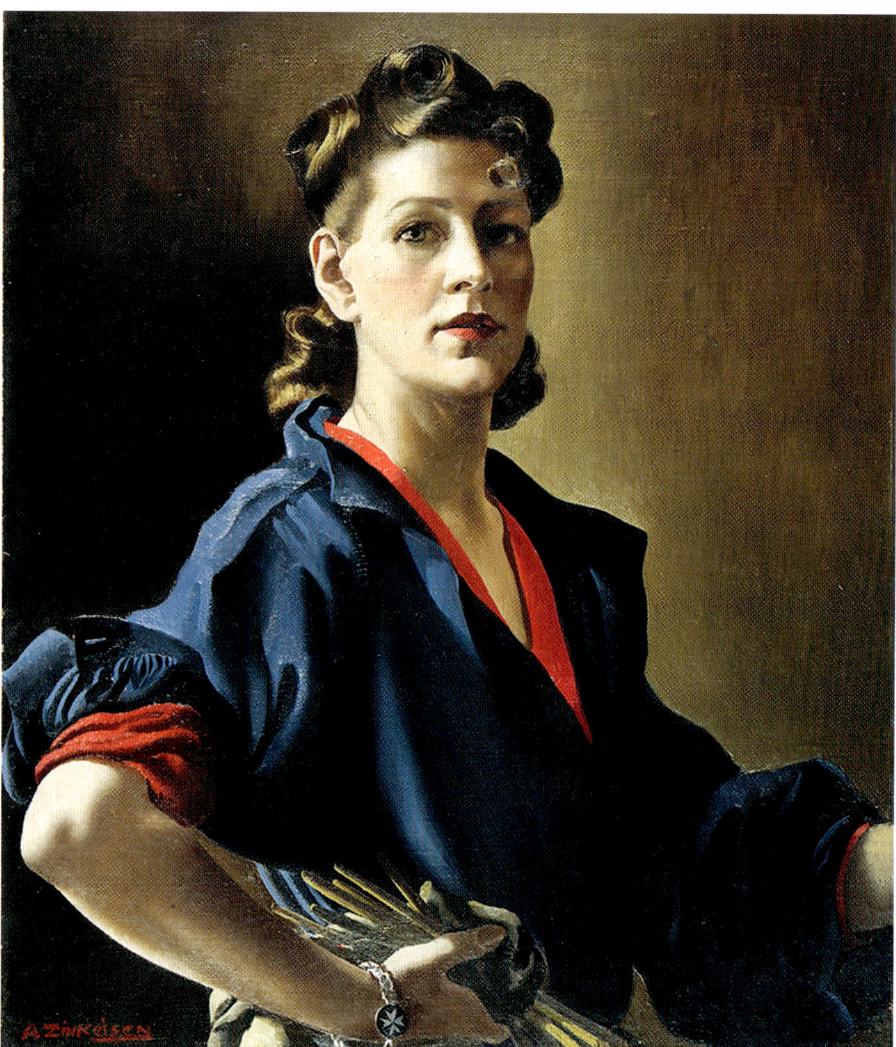

A.Zinkeisen

OPPOSITE
ANNA ZINKEISEN (1901–76)
Self-portrait, c.1944
Oil on canvas, 752 x 625mm
NPG 5884

RIGHT
GLUCK (1895–1978)
Self-portrait, 1942
Oil on canvas, 306 x 254mm
NPG 6462

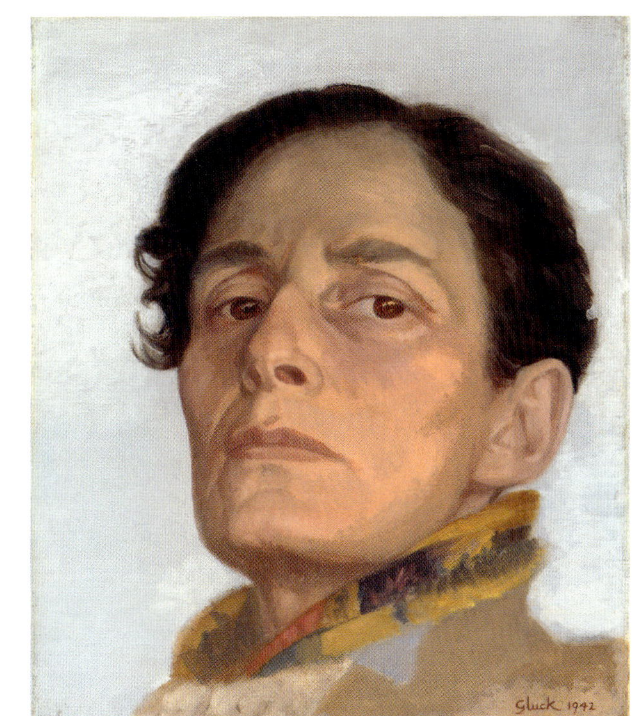

JULIE DRISCOLL (b.1947)

Steve Hiett, 1968

Chromogenic print, 250 x 378mm

NPG x132287

LULU (b.1948)

David Wedgbury, 1965

Cibachrome print, 280 x 280mm

NPG x76438

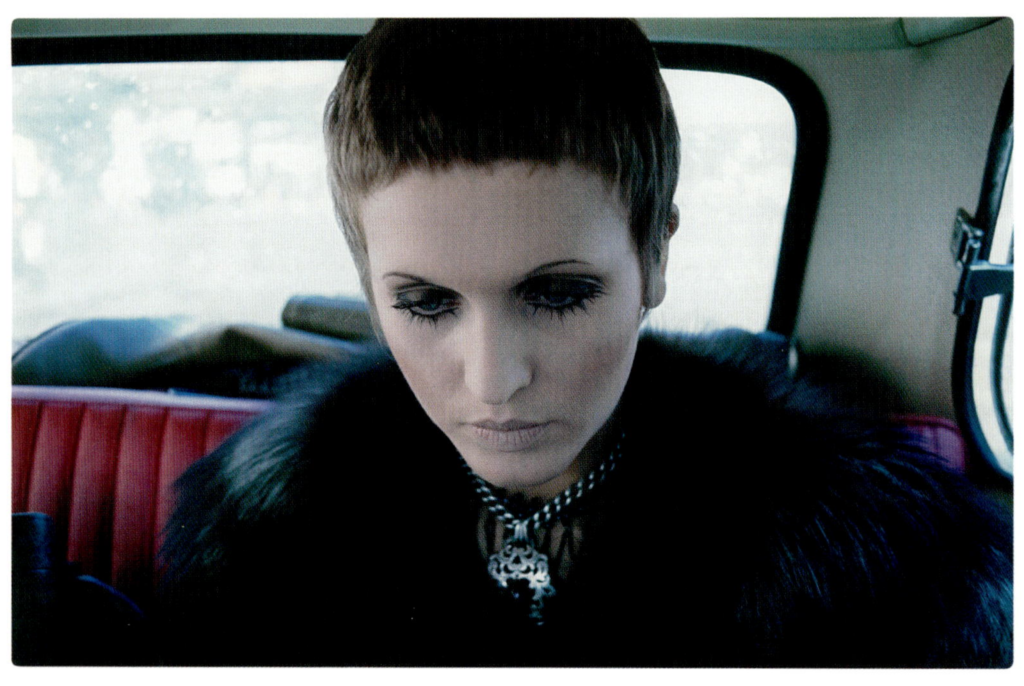

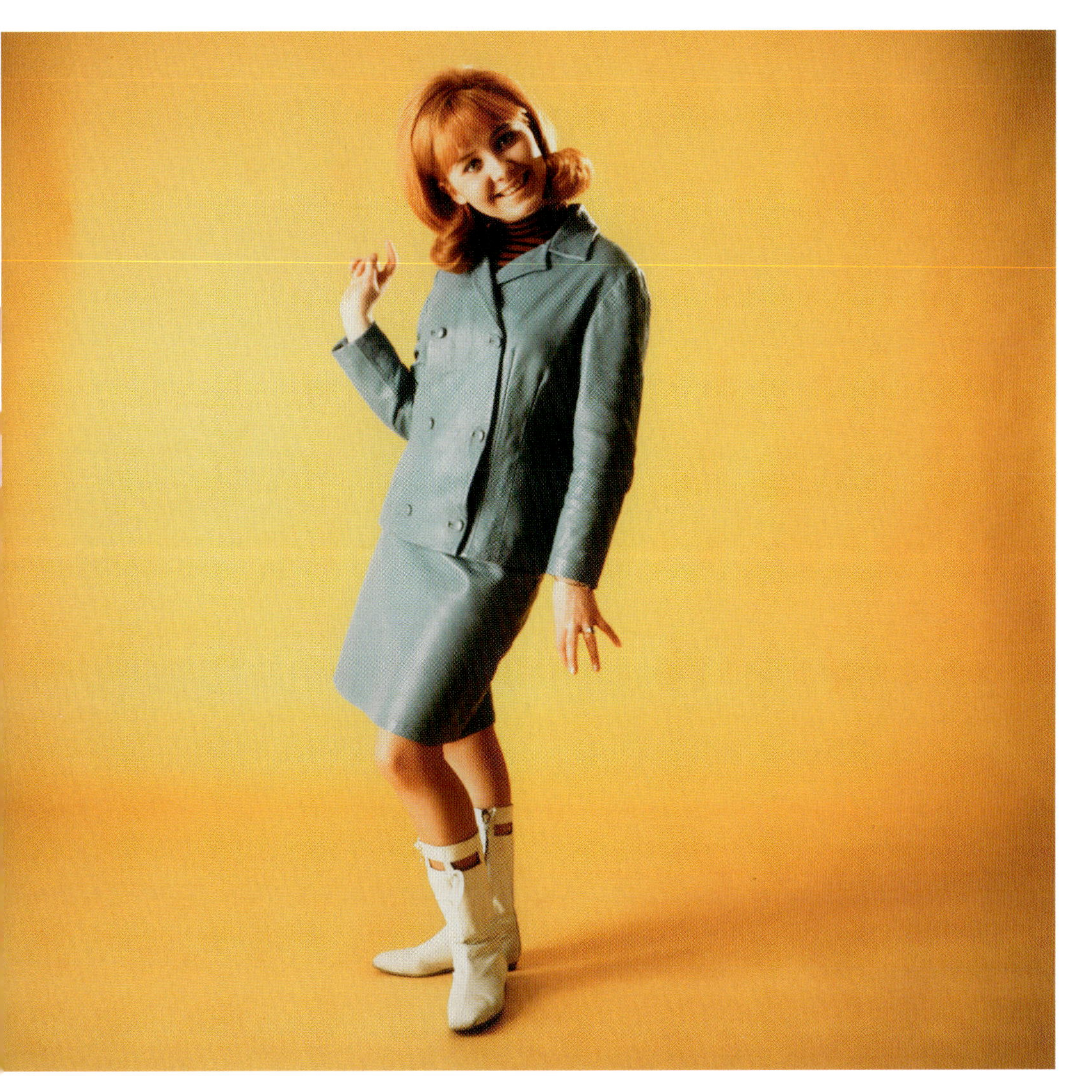

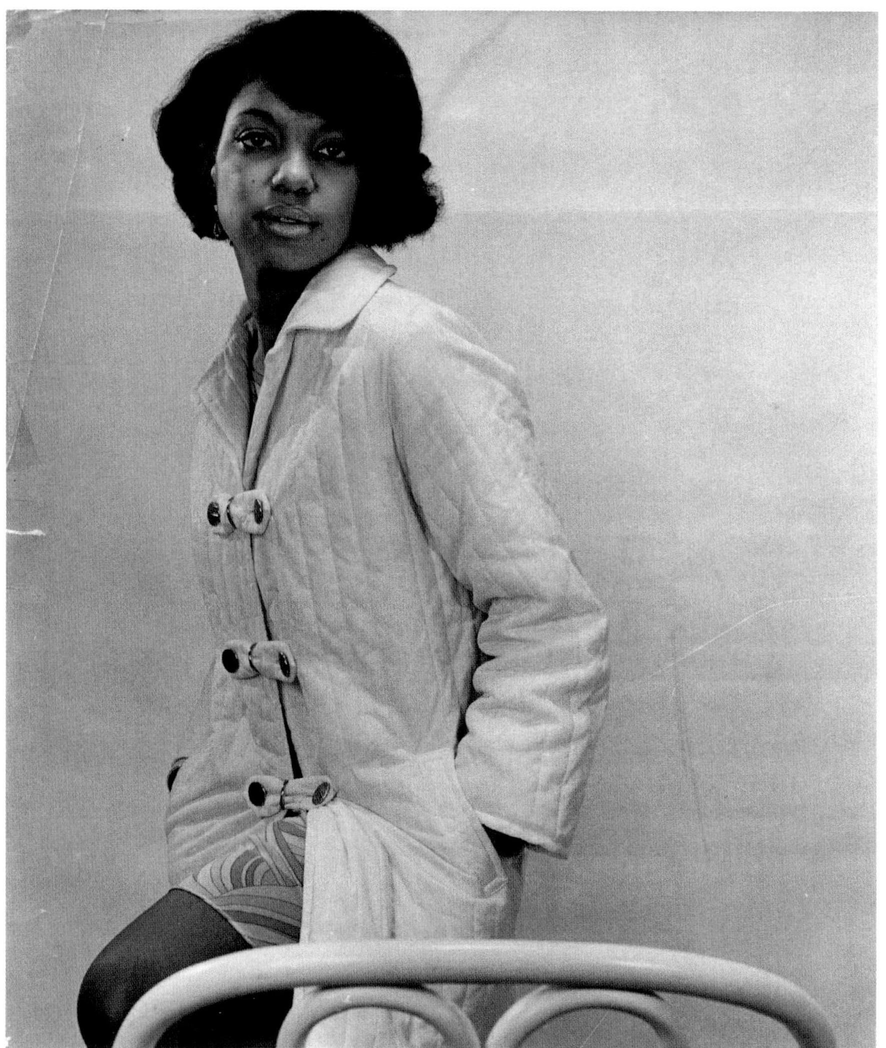

ERLIN IBRECK (b.1947)
James Barnor, 1967
Gelatin silver print, 295 x 246mm
NPG x200029

James Barnor (b.1929) worked as a
freelance photographer for South Africa's
Drum magazine after moving from Ghana
to London in 1959. *Drum* was an influential
anti-apartheid lifestyle and politics journal
– franchised across the African continent
and read by the black community in
London – which launched the career
of a number of photographers and models,
including cover star Erlin Ibreck. After
being spotted by Barnor queuing for a bus
outside London's Victoria station, Ibreck
enrolled at the Lucie Clayton modelling
school for two years, before changing
careers and moving to New York. Barnor's
photographs for *Drum* brought black models
into mainstream British media and captured
the experiences of the African diaspora
in 'Swinging Sixties' London.

QUEEN ELIZABETH II (b.1926)
Eve Arnold, 1968
Cibachrome print, 432 x 295mm
NPG P520

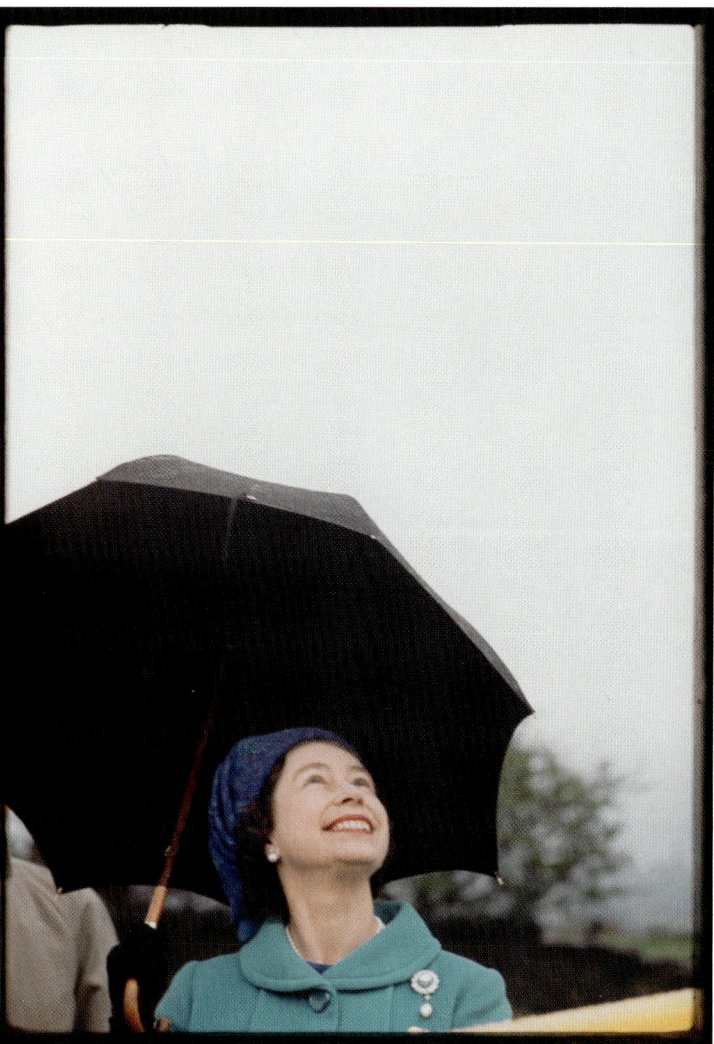

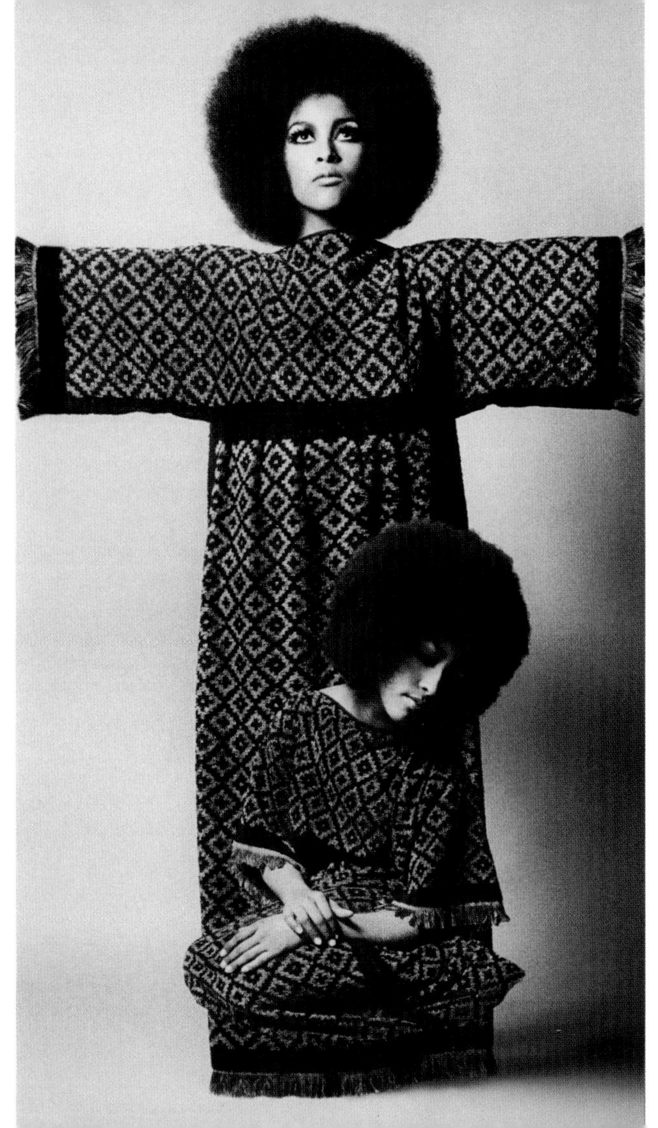

MARSHA HUNT (b.1947)
Horace Ové, 1968
Inkjet print, 532 x 284mm
NPG x126726

KAREN ELSON (b.1979)

(*Elson Street*)

Elaine Constantine, 2005

Chromogenic print, 378 x 473mm

NPG x131419

British supermodel and singer Karen
Elson has appeared in catwalk shows and
advertising campaigns for leading fashion
houses and on the covers of magazines
including *Vogue*, *W* and *Numero*. In 2005,
she won the British Fashion Award for
Model of the Year and she has built a
successful music career over a number
of years. *Elson Street*, commissioned
by *Pop* magazine, saw the photographer
and model return to their hometown of
Manchester. Elaine Constantine (b.1965)
became one of the defining image makers
for *The Face* and Italian and American
Vogue in the 1990s and is renowned for her
jubilant portrayals of British youth culture.

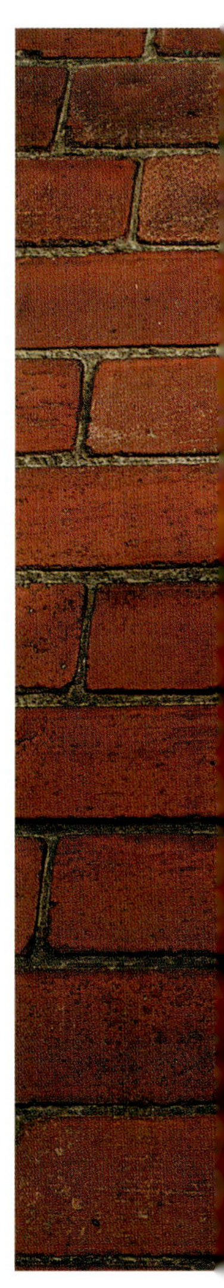

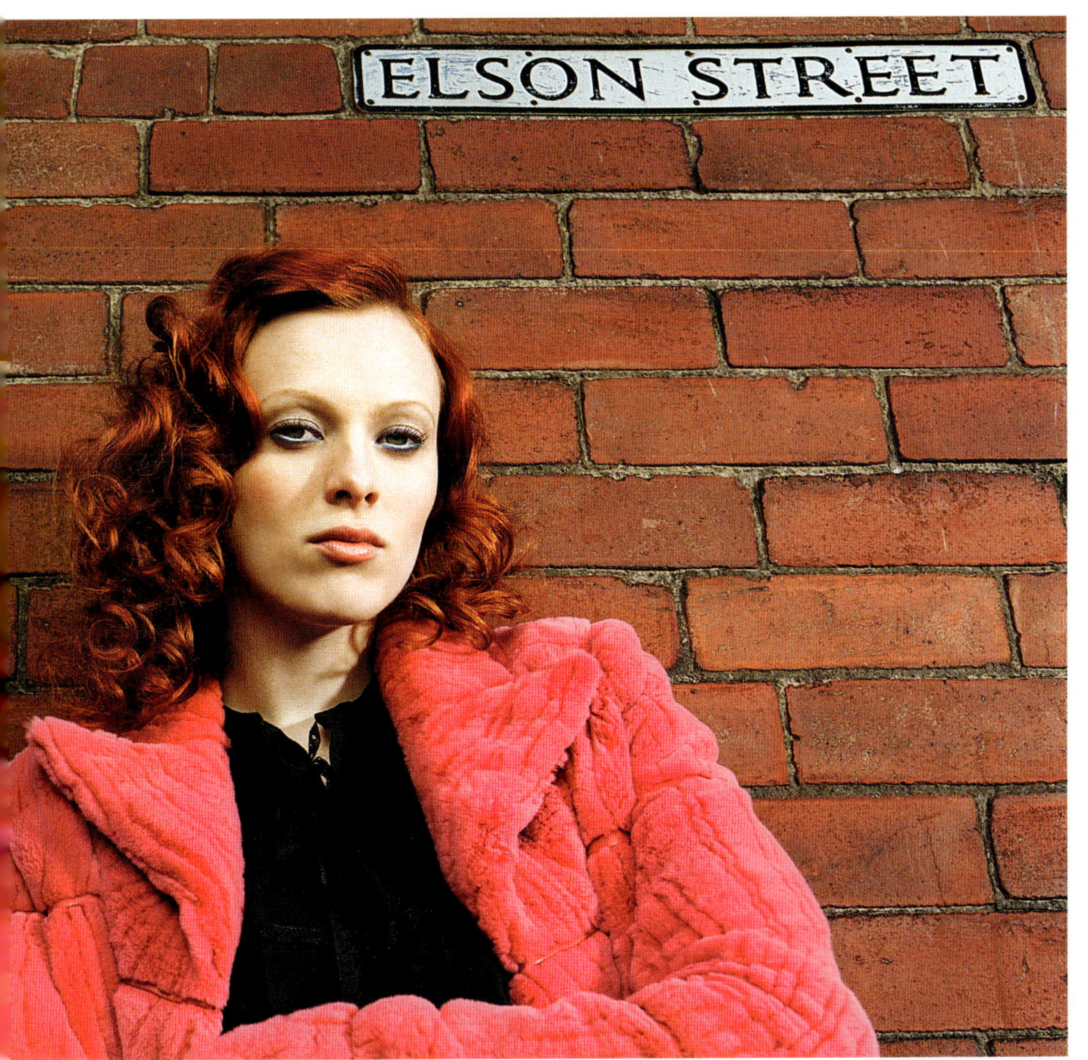

ELSON STREET

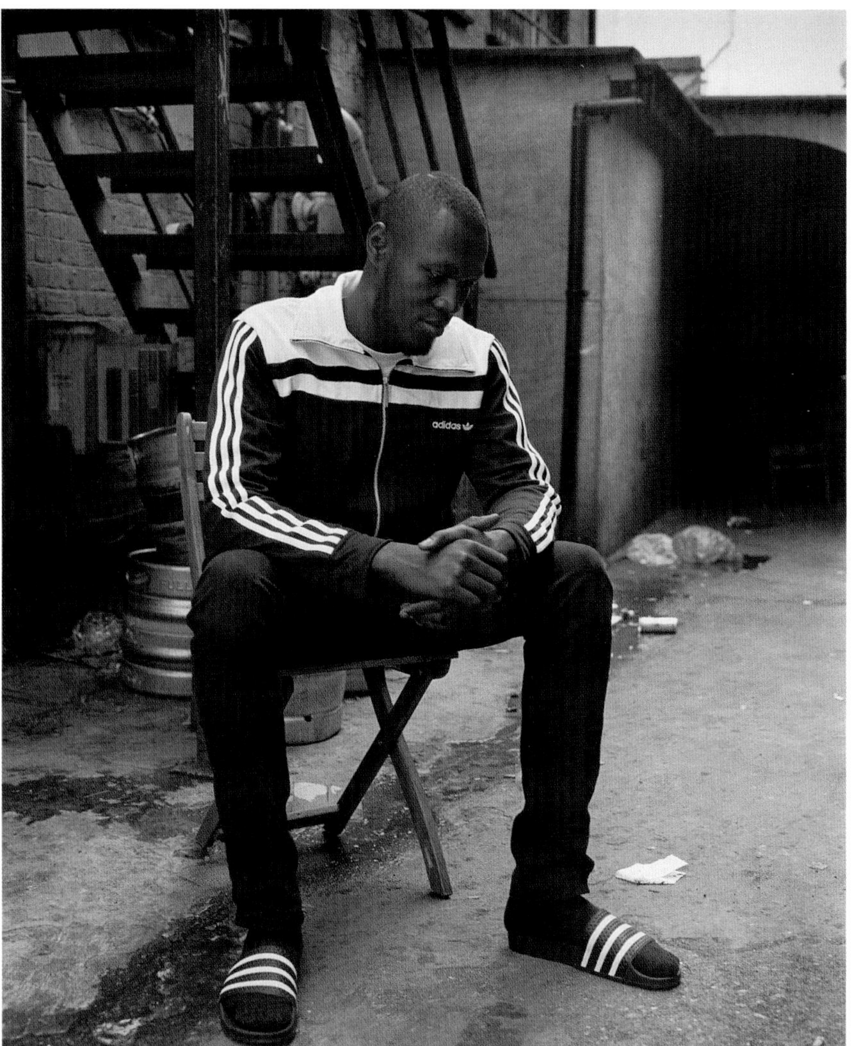

STORMZY (b.1993)
Olivia Rose, 2016
Gelatin silver print, 295 x 252mm
NPG x200706

MAISIE WILLIAMS (b.1997)
Miles Aldridge, 2017
Chromogenic print, 510 x 380mm
NPG x200784

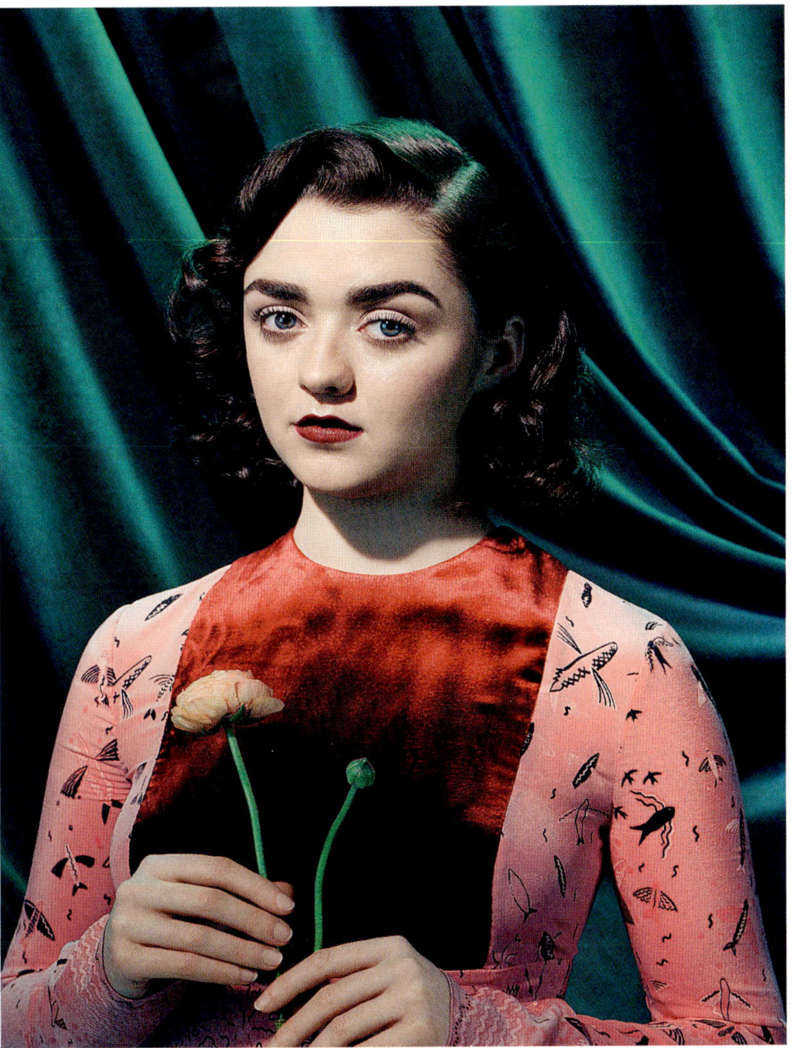

FASHION ICONS

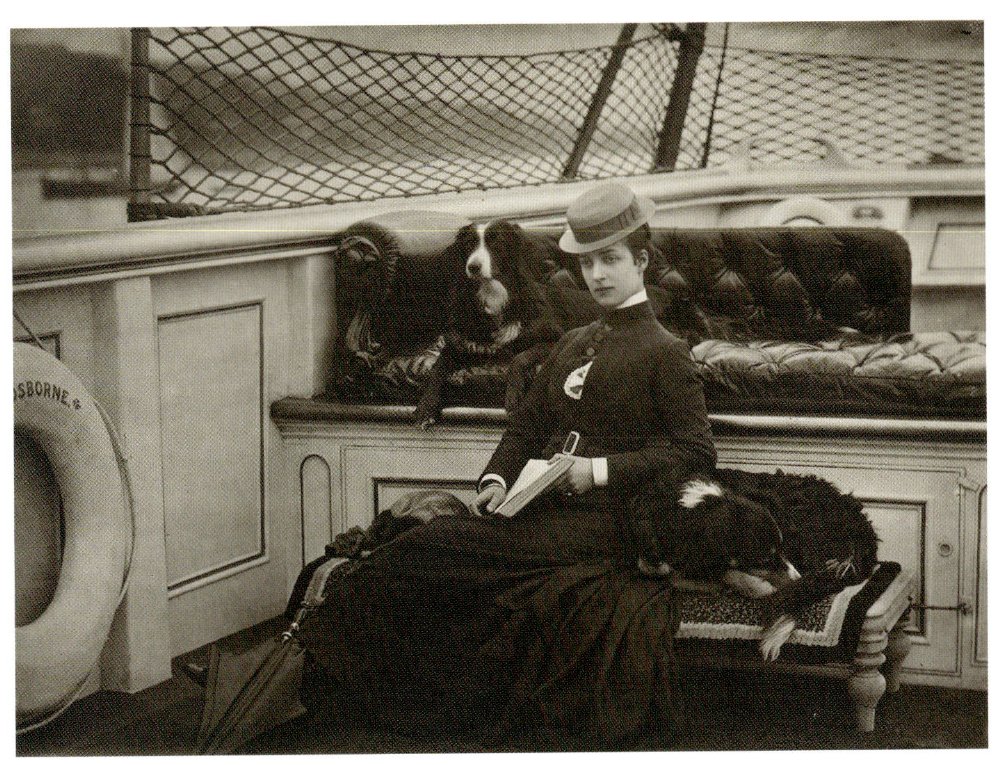

QUEEN ALEXANDRA (1844–1925)

Symonds & Co, 1877

Carbon print, 270 x 355mm

NPG x17460

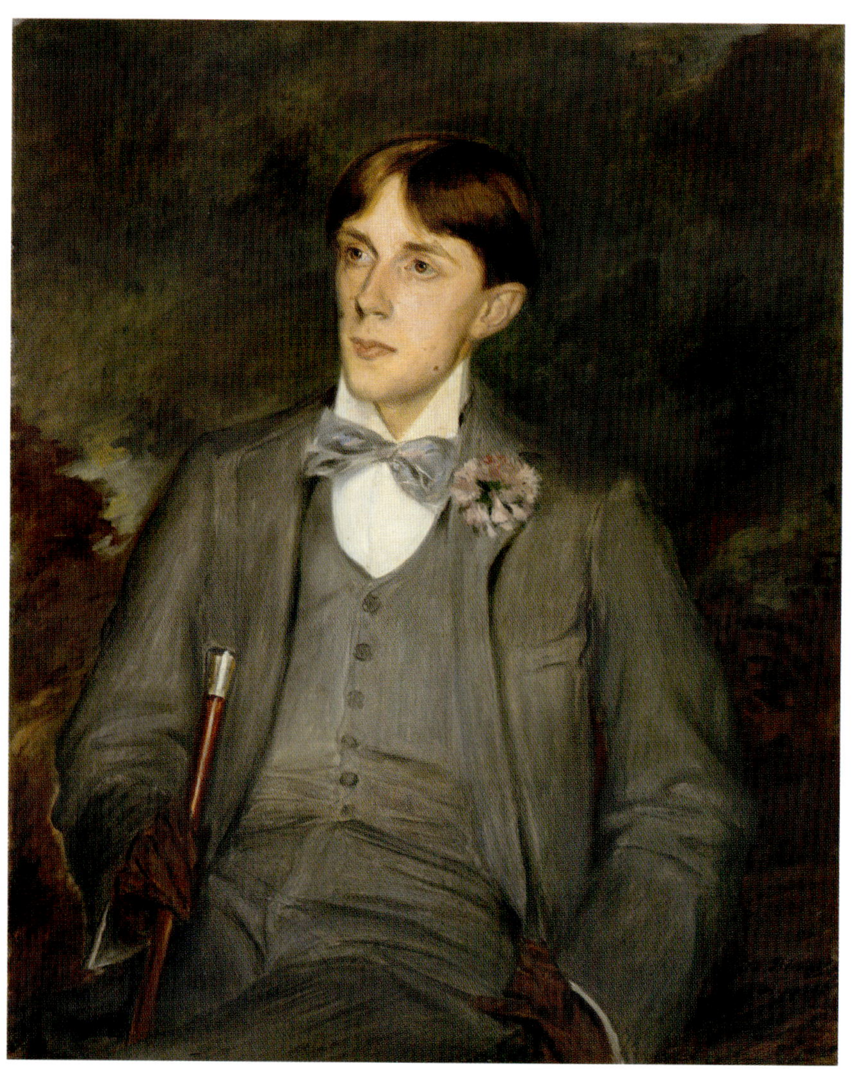

OPPOSITE

AUBREY BEARDSLEY (1827–98)

Jacques-Emile Blanche, 1895

Oil on canvas, 926 x 737mm

NPG 1991

RIGHT

VESTA TILLEY (1864–1952)

Published by Rotary Photographic Co Ltd,
1900s

Gelatin silver postcard print, 138 x 85mm

NPG Ax160041

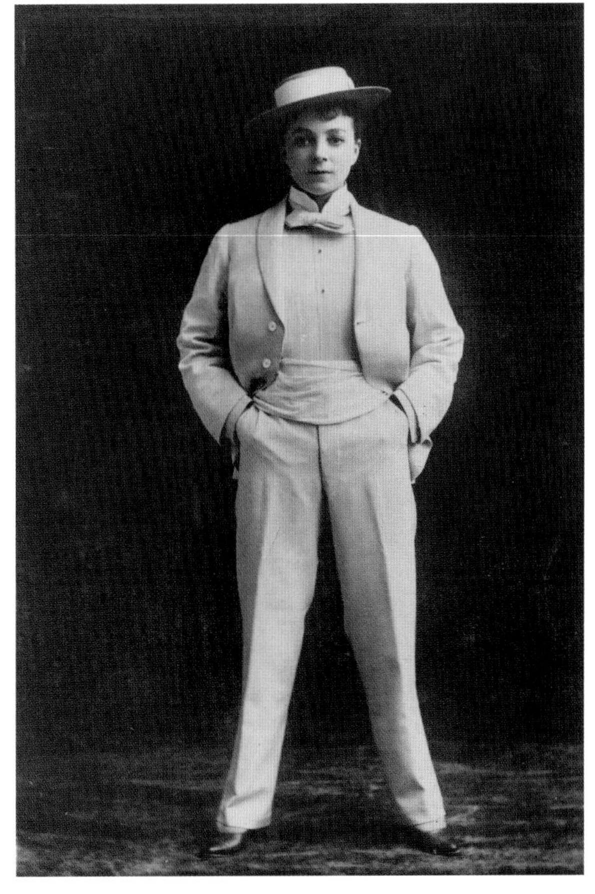

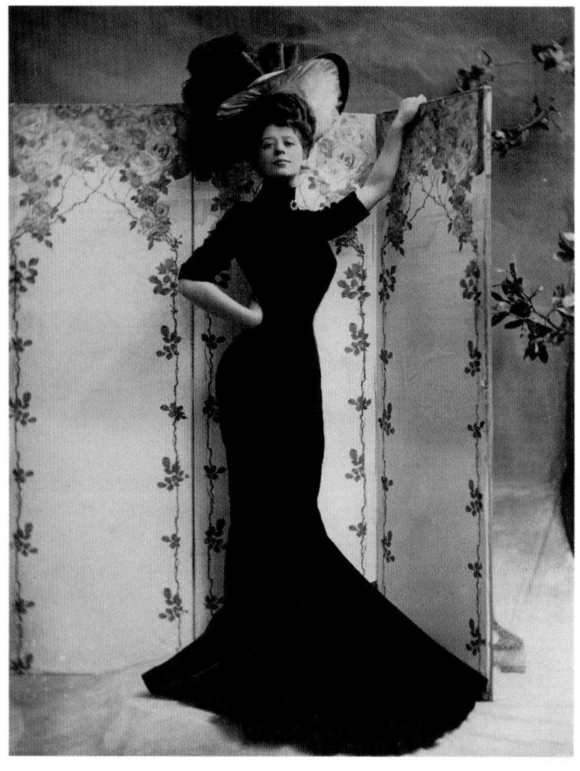

CAMILLE CLIFFORD (1888–1970)

Bassano Ltd, 1906

Gelatin silver print, 204 x 152mm

NPG x83027

Camille Clifford, known as 'The Gibson Girl', was a popular Edwardian actress whose nickname derived from her resemblance to the women drawn by the American artist Charles Dana Gibson (1867–1944). She first came to London in 1904 and two years later played the Duchess of Dunmow in Leslie Stuart's *The Belle of Mayfair*. Alexander Bassano's (1829–1913) studio photographed Clifford in the same year at 25 Old Bond Street. Her statuesque appearance is emphasised here by her full coiffure, plumed hat and sweeping train. The 'S' shape of her silhouette is accentuated by a tight corset, resulting in an exaggeration of feminine curves.

OPPOSITE

JOSEPHINE BAKER (1906–75)

Murray Korman, 1936

Gelatin silver print, 253 x 200mm

NPG x135816

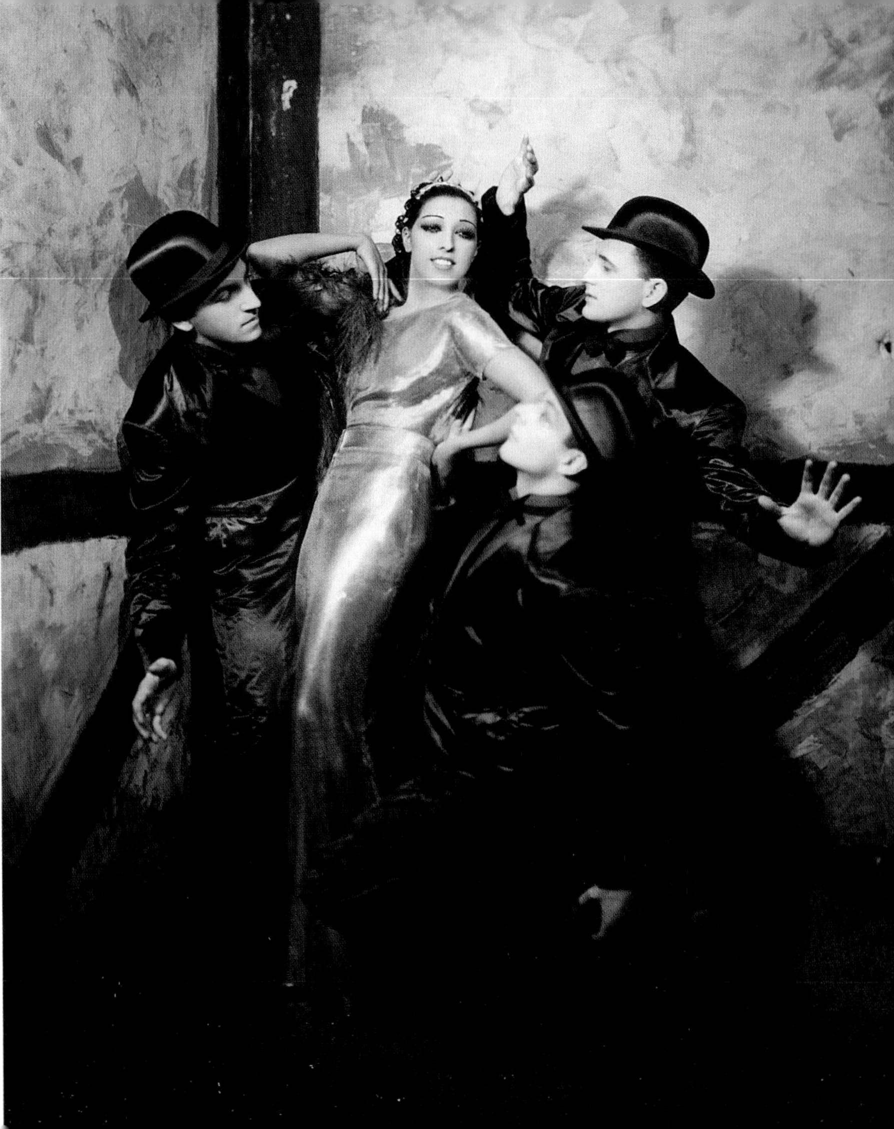

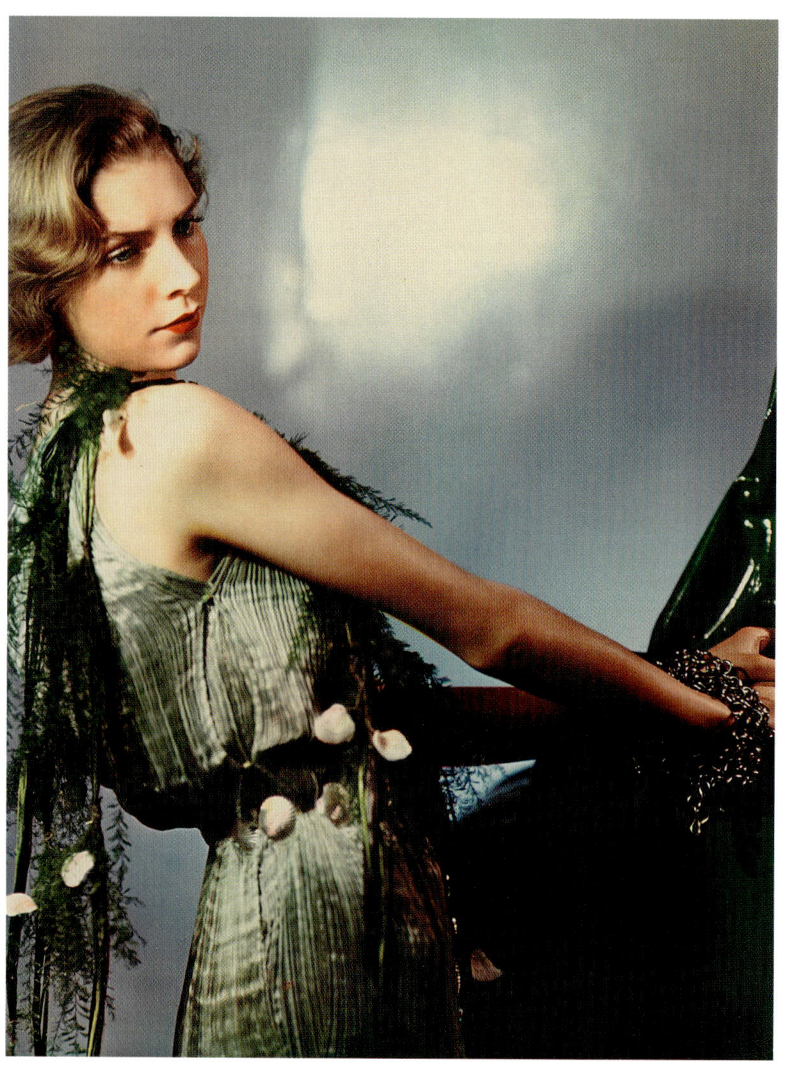

MRS RICHARD HART-DAVIS AS
ANDROMEDA
Madame Yevonde, 1935
Vivex colour print, 375 x 271mm
NPG x32989

This photograph is part of Madame
Yevonde's (1893–1975) much-celebrated
Goddesses and others series, which was
exhibited in July 1935 to launch her new
studio in Berkeley Square, London. The
society lady Mrs Richard Hart-Davis
plays the role of Andromeda, who, in
Greek mythology, is rescued from the sea
monster by Perseus. Hart-Davis is dressed
in a cascading Marià Fortuny (1871–1949)
dress with pearlescent ripples evocative
of the sea, and an intricate shawl made
to resemble seaweed, embellished with
shells handmade by Yevonde and her
assistants. Contrary to many art historical
depictions of the goddess as a helpless
maiden, Yevonde's Andromeda appears
defiant, wearing a bold red lip and soft
finger-wave hairstyle popular among
modern women of the 1930s.

WALLIS, DUCHESS
OF WINDSOR (1896–1986)
Dorothy Wilding, 1935
Chlorobromide print, 359 x 404mm
NPG P870(15)

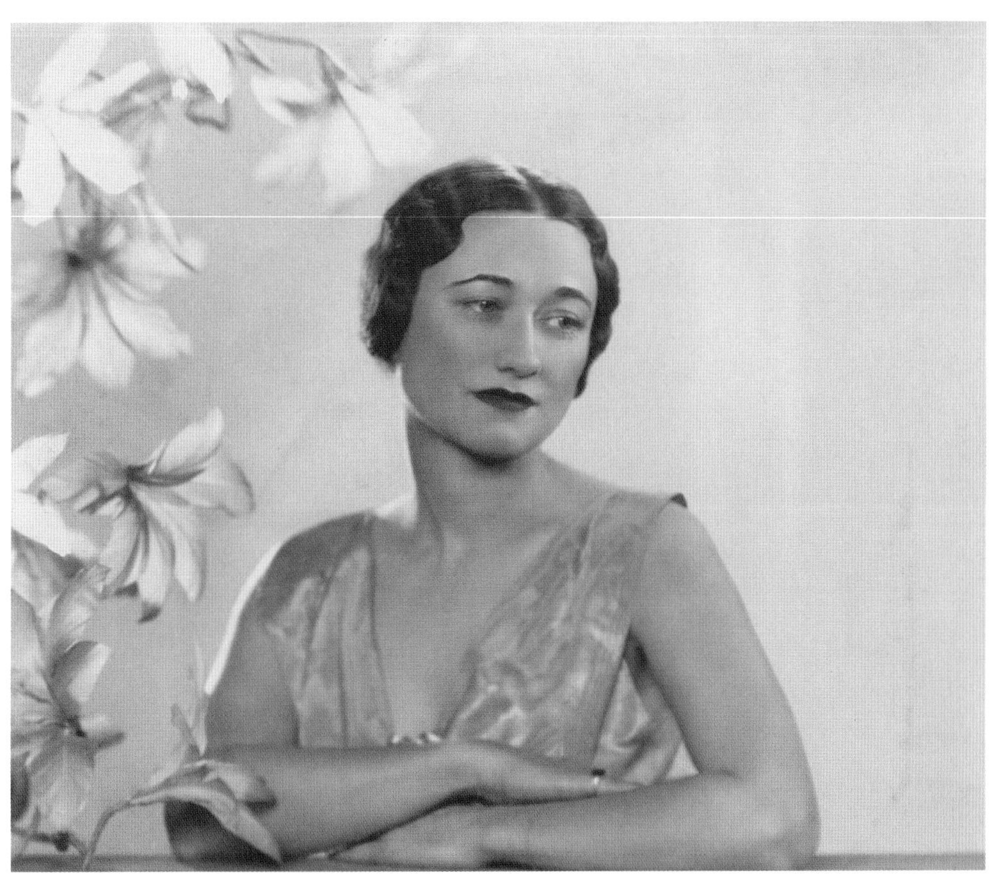

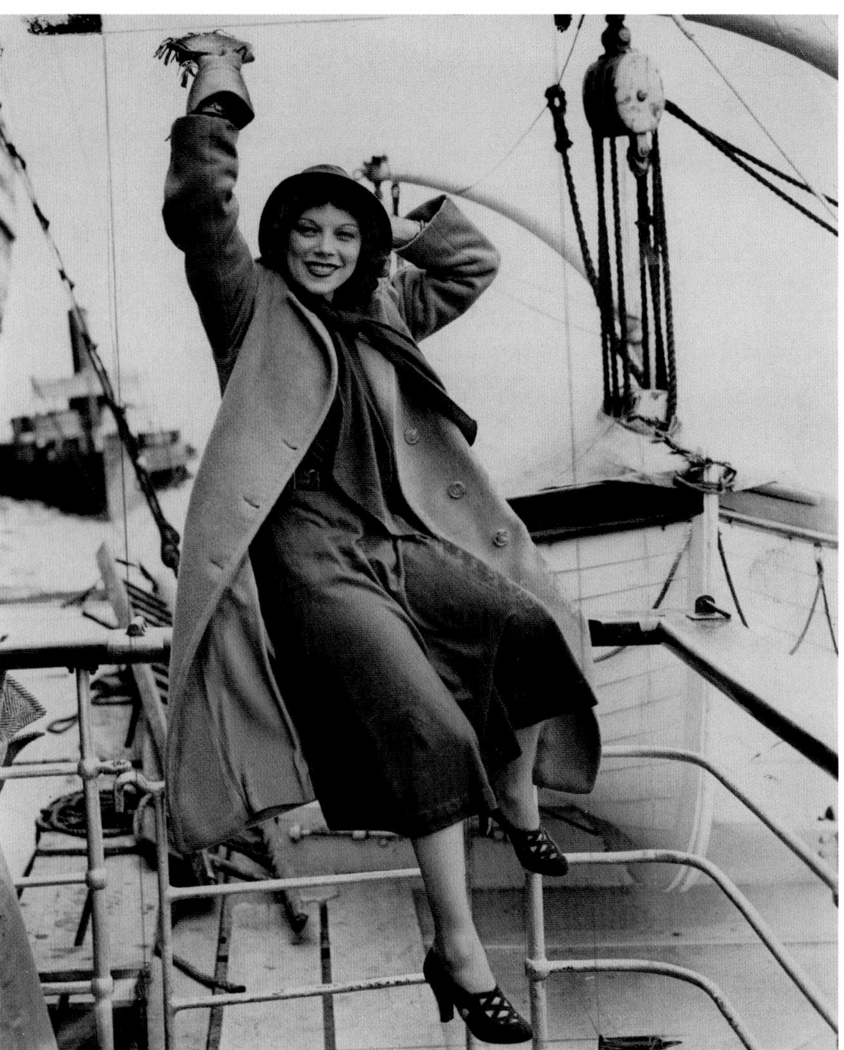

OPPOSITE

TILLY LOSCH (1907–75)

Planet News, 1938

Gelatin silver press print, 240 x 190mm

NPG x184085

RIGHT

WENDA PARKINSON (1923–87)

Norman Parkinson, 1950

Colour print on card mount, 485 x 330mm

NPG x30103

In a career that spanned seven decades, Norman Parkinson (1913–90) was celebrated for his inventiveness as a fashion photographer. Parkinson first met Wenda Rogerson (1923–87) when she appeared as a young actress at the Arts Theatre Club, supplementing her salary through modelling. She became his model and they married in 1947. In this image for *Vogue*, Wenda wears a tailored lime-yellow Moygashel straight jacket and skirt with floppy bow blouse by Hardy Amies (1909–2003), Erik cloche hat and Rayne shoes to match.

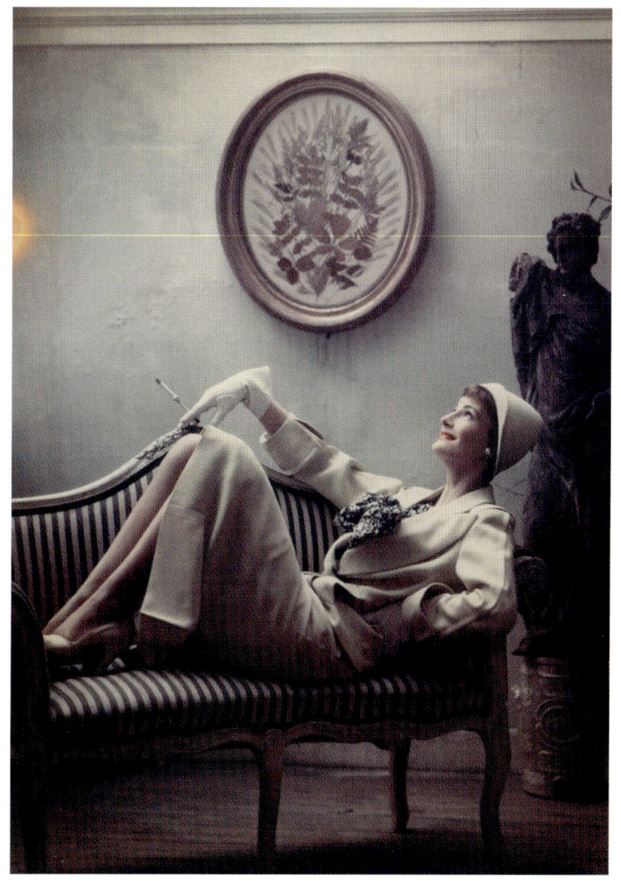

JEANNIE PATCHETT (1926–2002)
Norman Parkinson, 1950
Chromogenic print, 482 x 376mm
NPG x30098

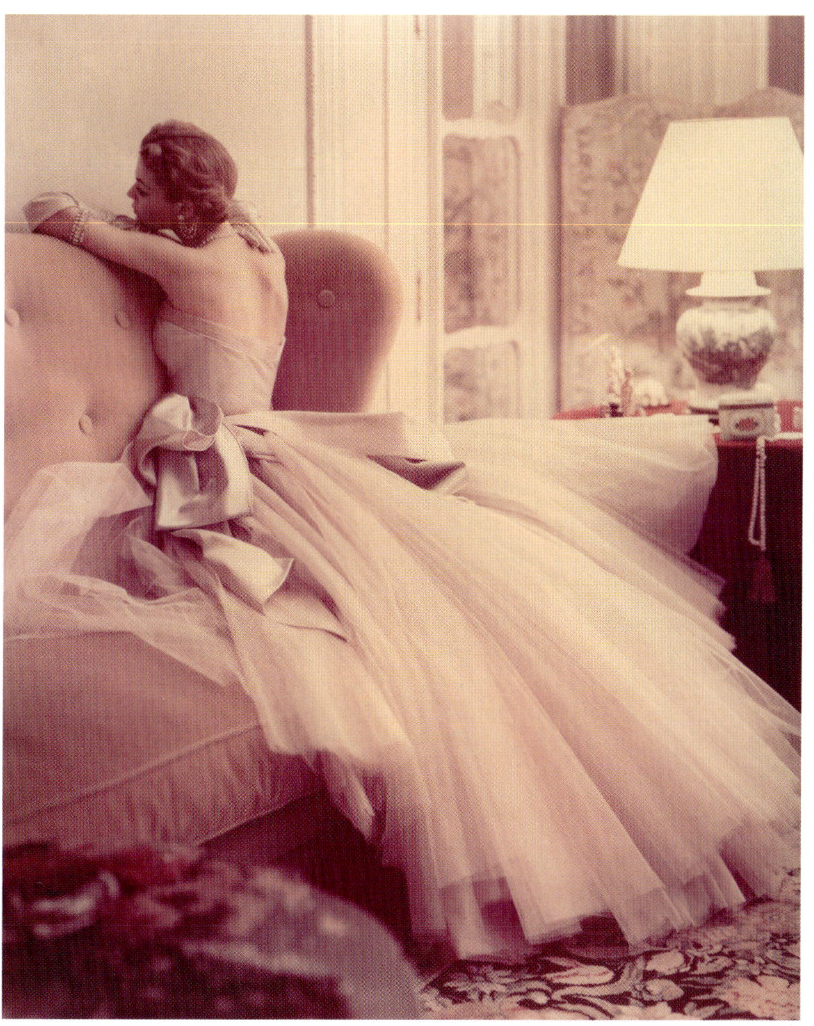

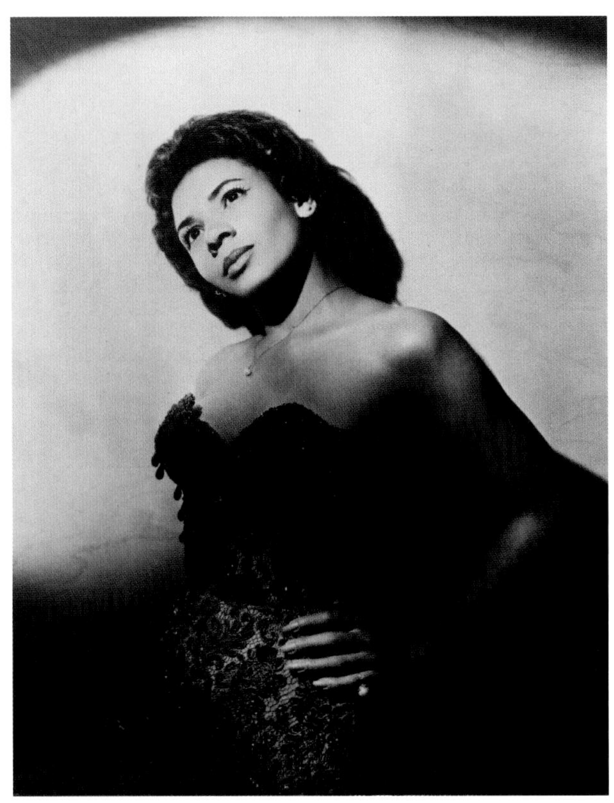

LEFT
DAME SHIRLEY BASSEY (b.1937)
Angus McBean, 1959
Gelatin silver print, 355 x 270mm
NPG P885

OPPOSITE
AUDREY HEPBURN (1929–93)
Cecil Beaton, 1960
Gelatin silver print, 180 x 185mm
NPG x14103

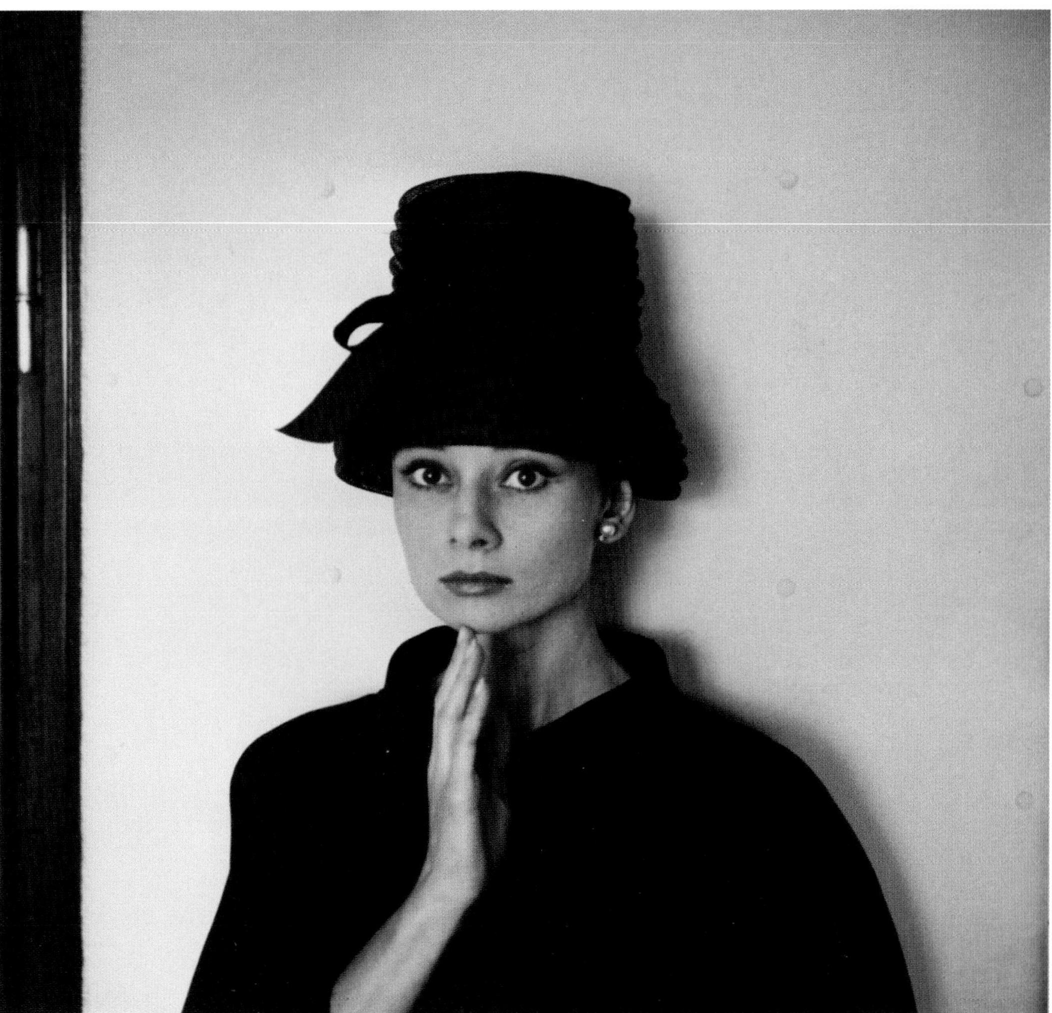

CHARLOTTE RAMPLING
(b.1946)
Lewis Morley, 1963
Cibachrome print, 293 x 393mm
NPG x87166

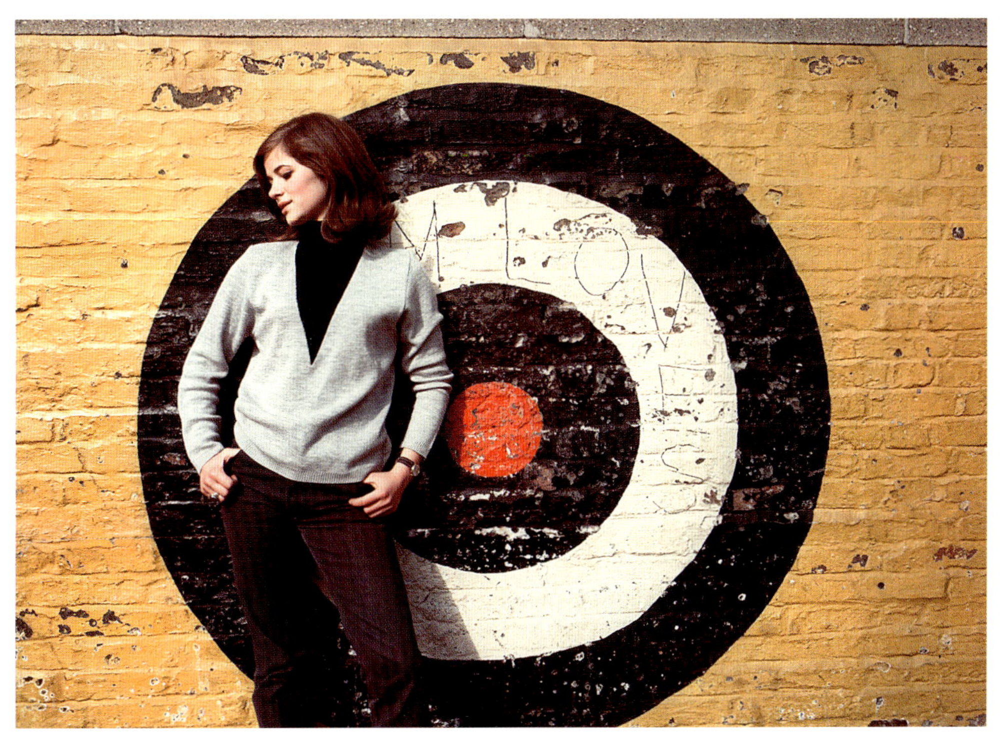

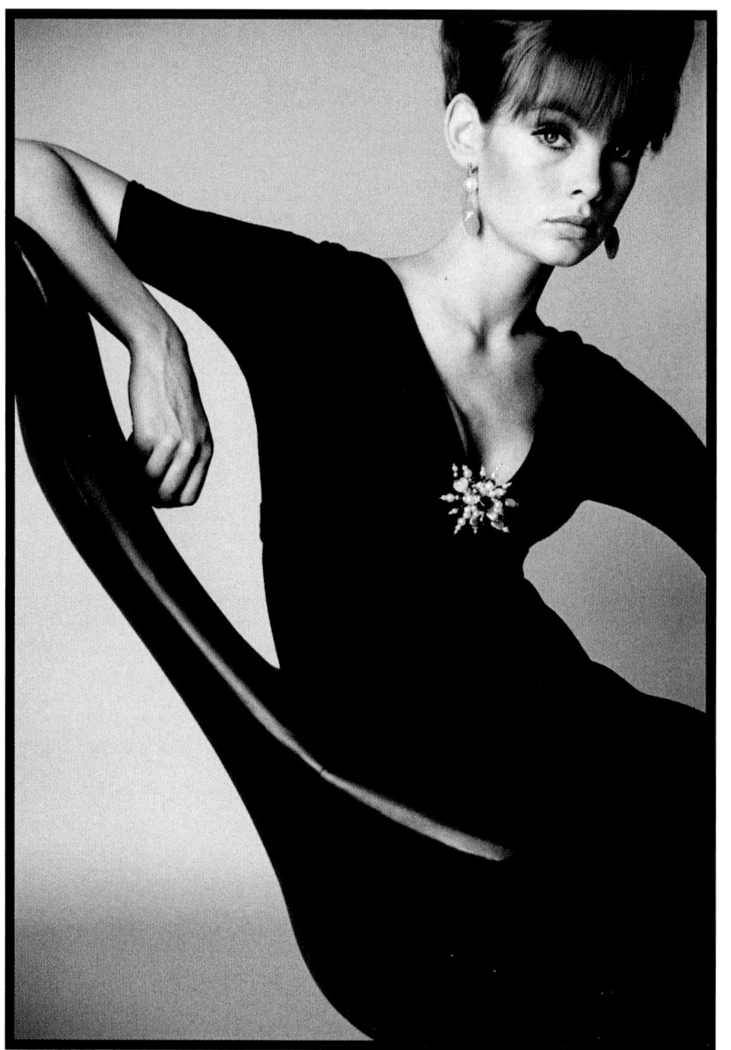

JEAN SHRIMPTON (b.1942)
David Bailey, 1963
Gelatin silver print, 508 x 344mm
NPG P954

David Bailey (b.1938) recalled first meeting model Jean Shrimpton (b.1942) in early 1961 on a Kellogg's Cornflakes photoshoot with Brian Duffy (1933–2010). Shrimpton's first modelling session with Bailey was on 12 April later that year for an Acrilan textile advertisement. It marked the beginning of the pair's frequent collaboration throughout the 1960s, which redefined fashion photography through dramatic lighting, composition and pose. This photograph was shot in Bailey's studio and a variant was published in the November 1963 issue of *Queen* magazine. Shrimpton wears an elegant fitted dress with a diamanté brooch, her figure enhanced against an elongated chair.

SIR RINGO STARR (b.1940),
JOHN LENNON (1940–80),
GEORGE HARRISON (1943–2001),
SIR PAUL MCCARTNEY (b.1942)
(*The Beatles*)
Robert Whitaker, 1964
Gelatin silver print, 400 x 379mm
NPG P1348

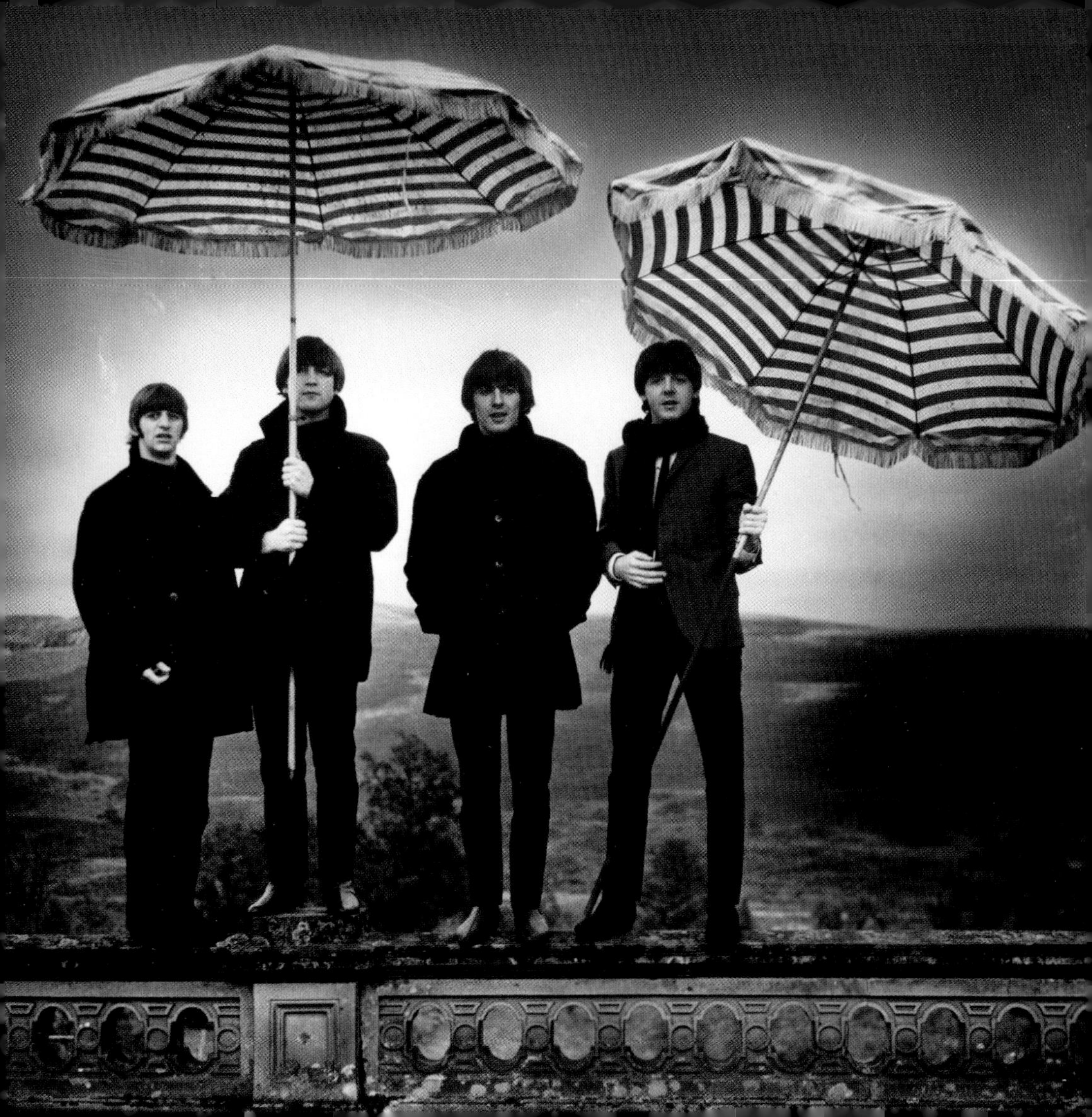

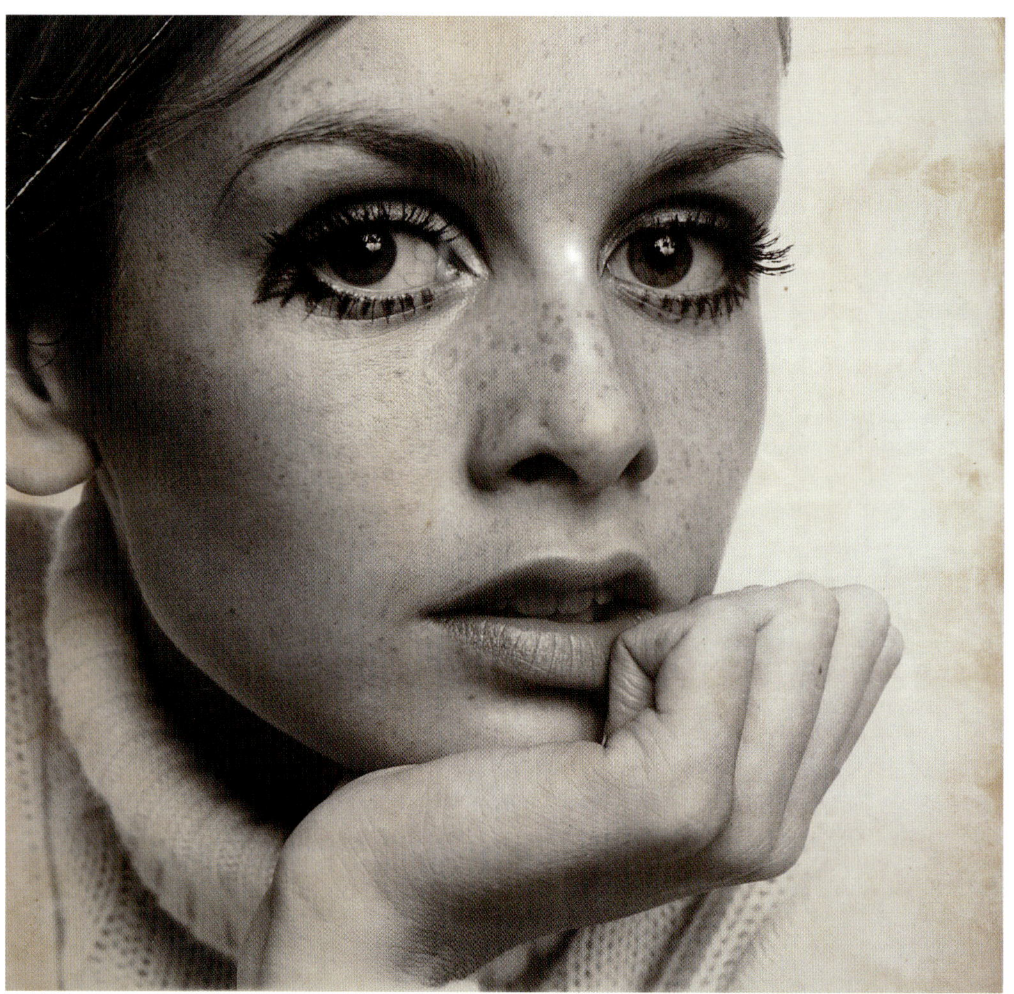

TWIGGY (b.1949)
Ronald Traeger, 1967
Cibachrome print, 430 x 355mm
NPG x125452

Dame Lesley Lawson (b.1949), best-
known as Twiggy, was named 'The
Face of 1966' in a *Daily Express* article
by journalist Deirdre McSharry and
arguably became the world's first
supermodel. With her dramatic eye
make-up, androgynous figure and short
haircut shaped by Leonard of Mayfair
and coloured by Daniel Galvin, Twiggy
embodied the 1960s look and influenced
a generation of young people. American
fashion photographer, artist and designer
Ronald Traeger (1936–68) photographed
Twiggy on numerous occasions. In this
close-up portrait, her cropped hairstyle
contrasts with her painted-on eyelashes
and freckles.

JIMI HENDRIX (1942–70)
Gered Mankowitz, 1967
Gelatin silver print, 430 x 423mm
NPG x126233

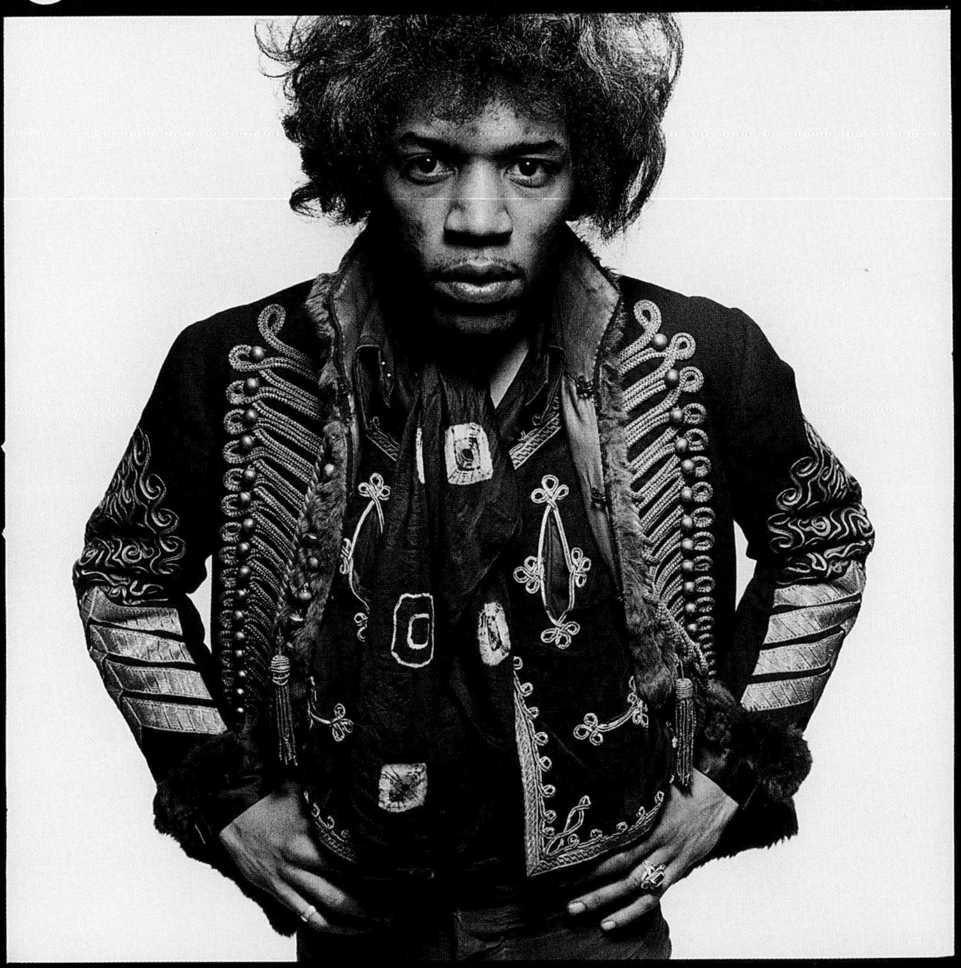

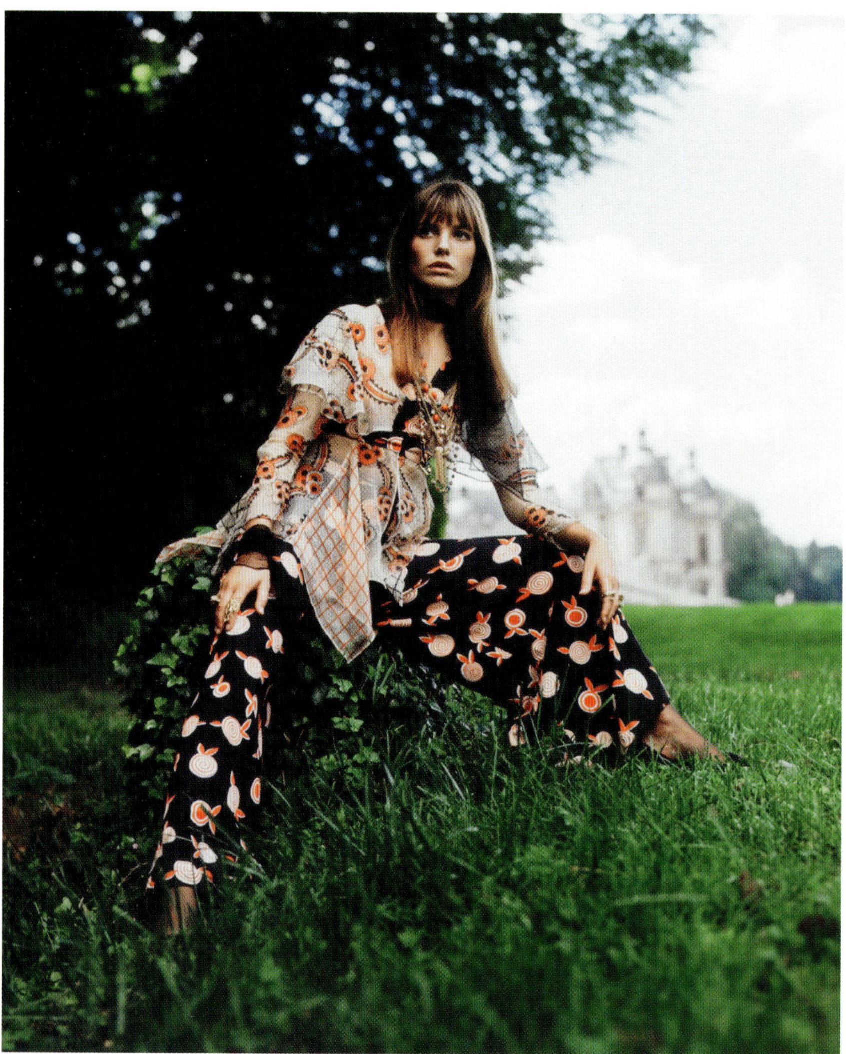

JANE BIRKIN (b.1946)
Patrick Lichfield, 1969
Inkjet print, 372 x 304mm
NPG x128496

Photographed for American *Vogue* in
Chantilly, France, the actress, singer and
model Jane Birkin (b.1946) wears a chiffon
top and wide crepe pants designed by Ossie
Clark (1942–96). Clark's flowing fabrics,
printed with his then-wife Celia Birtwell's
(b.1941) art deco inspired floral motifs,
created a romantic and feminine aesthetic.
The society and fashion photographer
Patrick Lichfield (1939–2005) was a cousin
of Queen Elizabeth II. Known for his
intimate portraits of the royal family,
Lichfield was also a chronicler of the
'Swinging Sixties'.

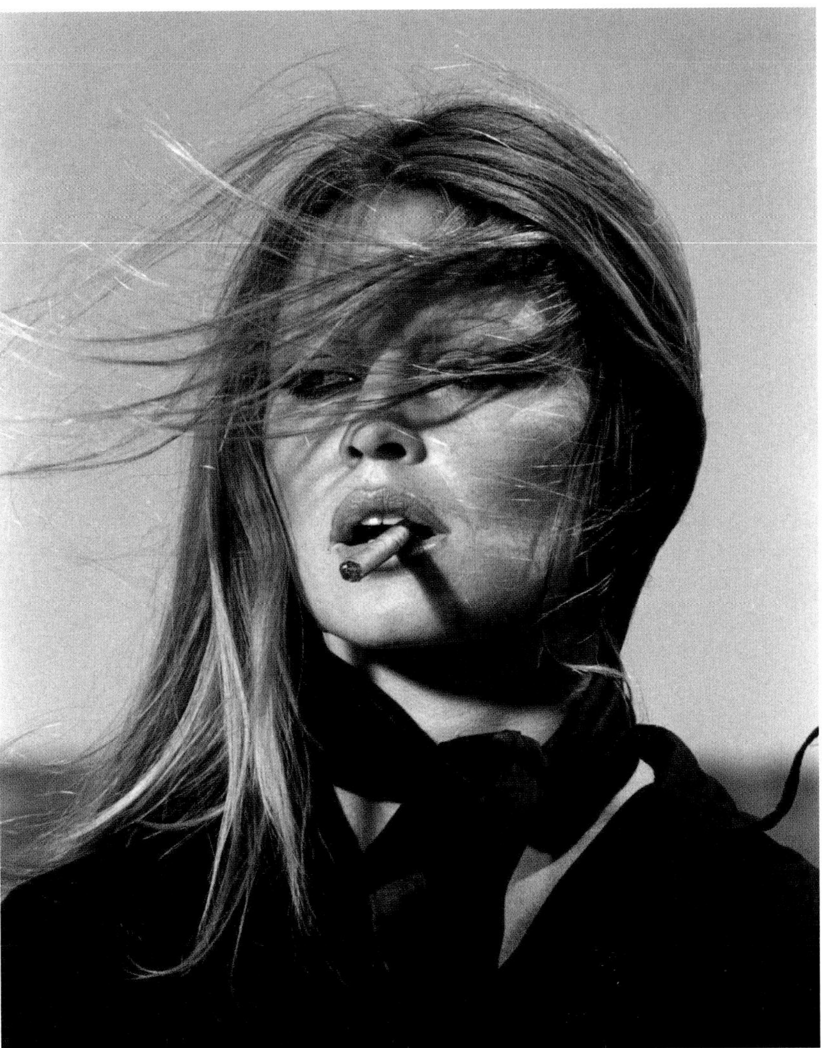

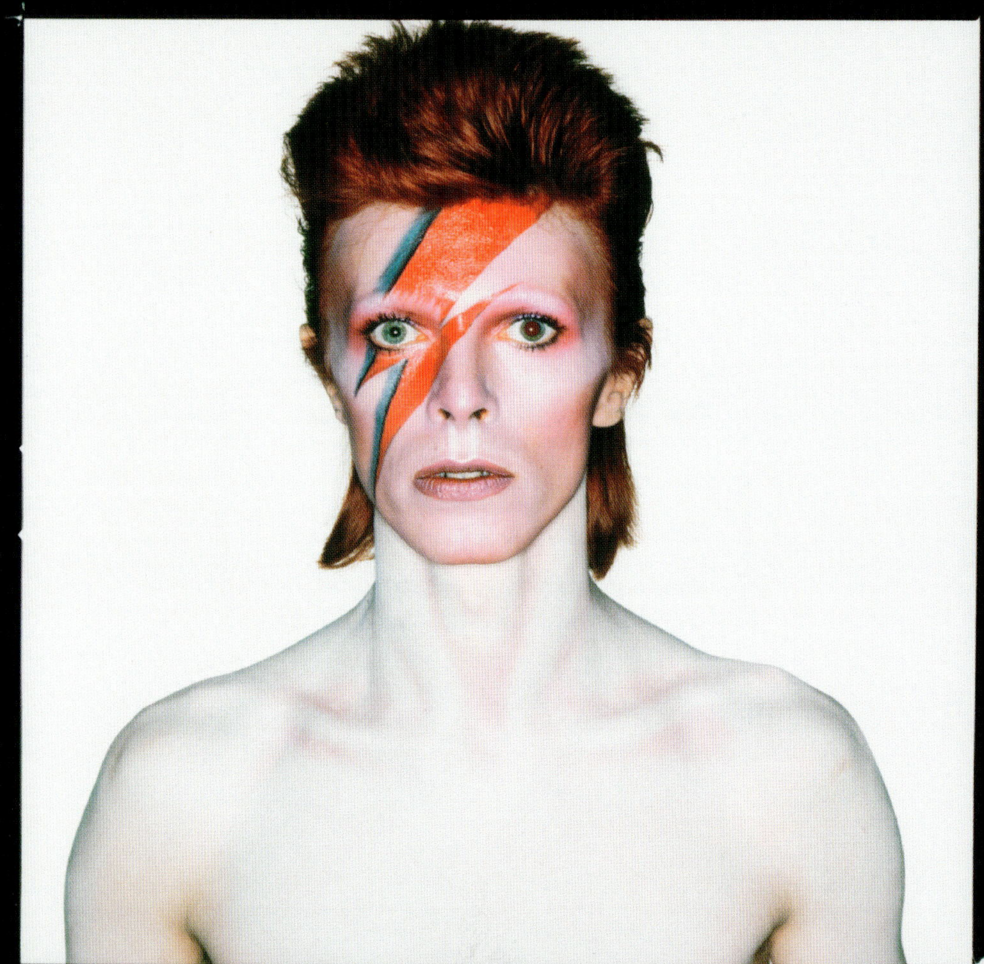

OPPOSITE

DAVID BOWIE (1947–2016)

Brian Duffy, 1973

Chromogenic print, 197 x197mm

NPG x137463

RIGHT

JERRY HALL (b.1956)

Norman Parkinson, 1976

Chromogenic print, 511 x 408mm

NPG x30182

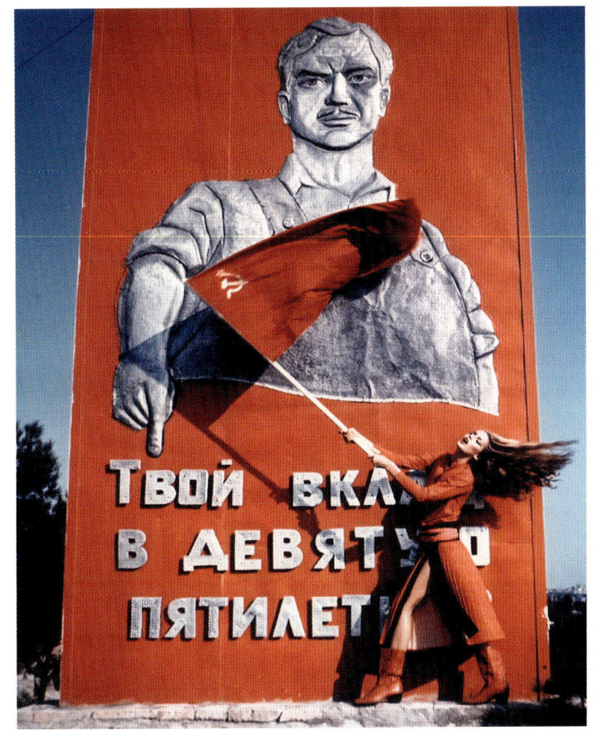

ТВОЙ ВКЛА
В ДЕВЯТ
ПЯТИЛЕТ

TROJAN (1966–86) and LEIGH
BOWERY (1961–94)
David Gwinnutt, 1983
Gelatin silver print, 480 x 342mm
NPG X131399

David Gwinnutt (b.1961) encountered the
iconic performance artist Leigh Bowery
outside Heaven nightclub in Charing
Cross, London, and remembered being
enthralled by his experimental dress
sense. Gwinnutt photographed Bowery
at his home in east London, which he
shared with the artist Trojan. Immersed
in the hedonistic London underground
club scene – in which a new wave of
artists, designers and musicians flourished
and collaborated – Bowery and Trojan
used their bodies as a canvas for creative
expression with outlandish outfits and
theatrical make-up, including Trojan's
painted 'Picasso face' depicted in this
portrait. In January 1985, Bowery launched
the Taboo club in Leicester Square,
instructing visitors to follow his mantra:
'Dress as though your life depends on
it or don't bother.'

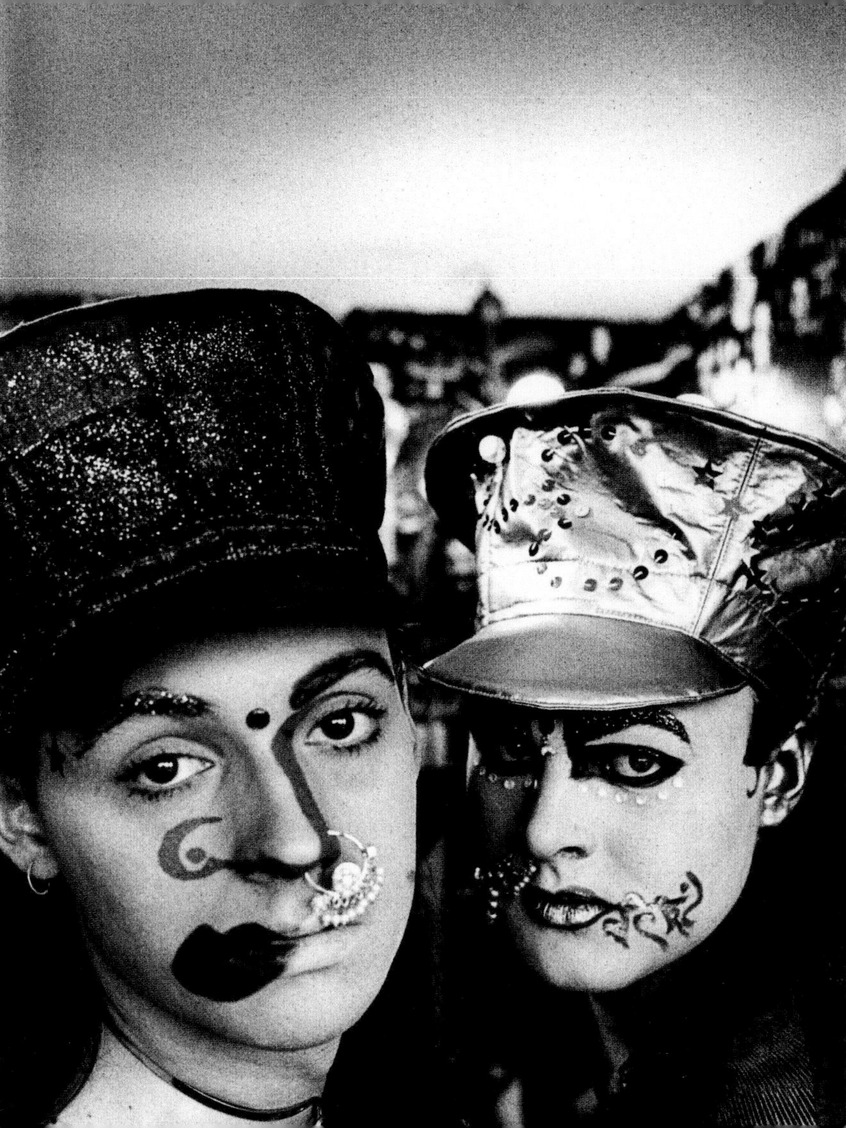

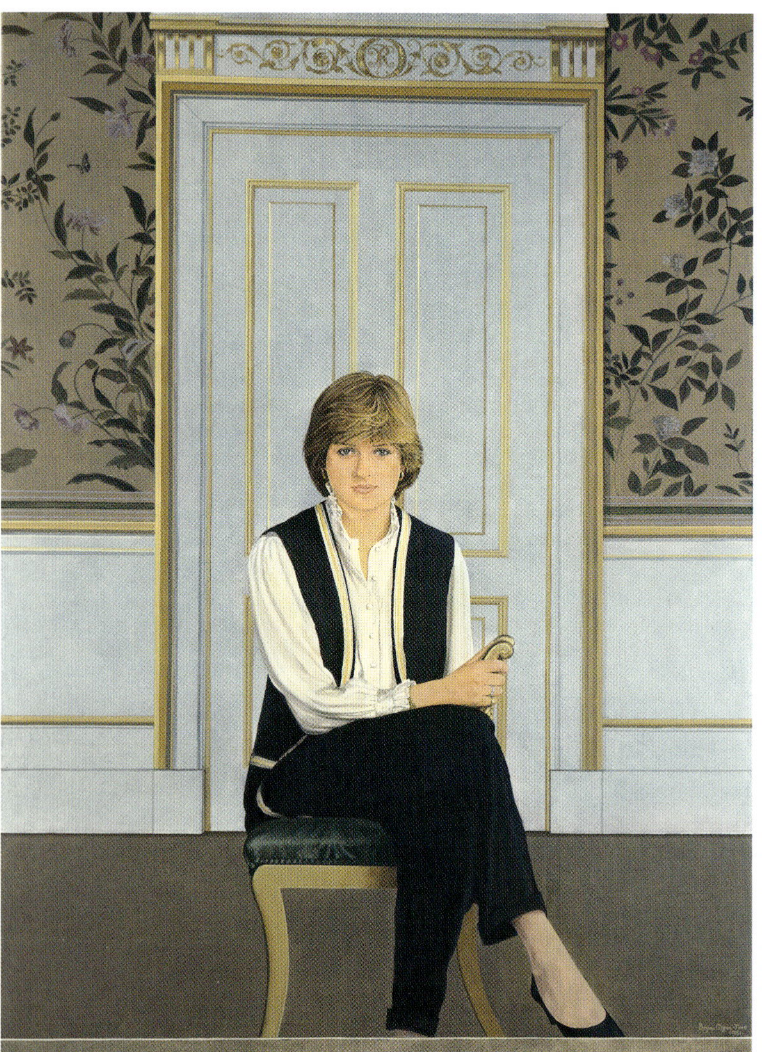

DIANA, PRINCESS OF WALES
(1961–97)
Bryan Organ, 1981
Acrylic on canvas, 1778 x 1270mm
NPG 5408

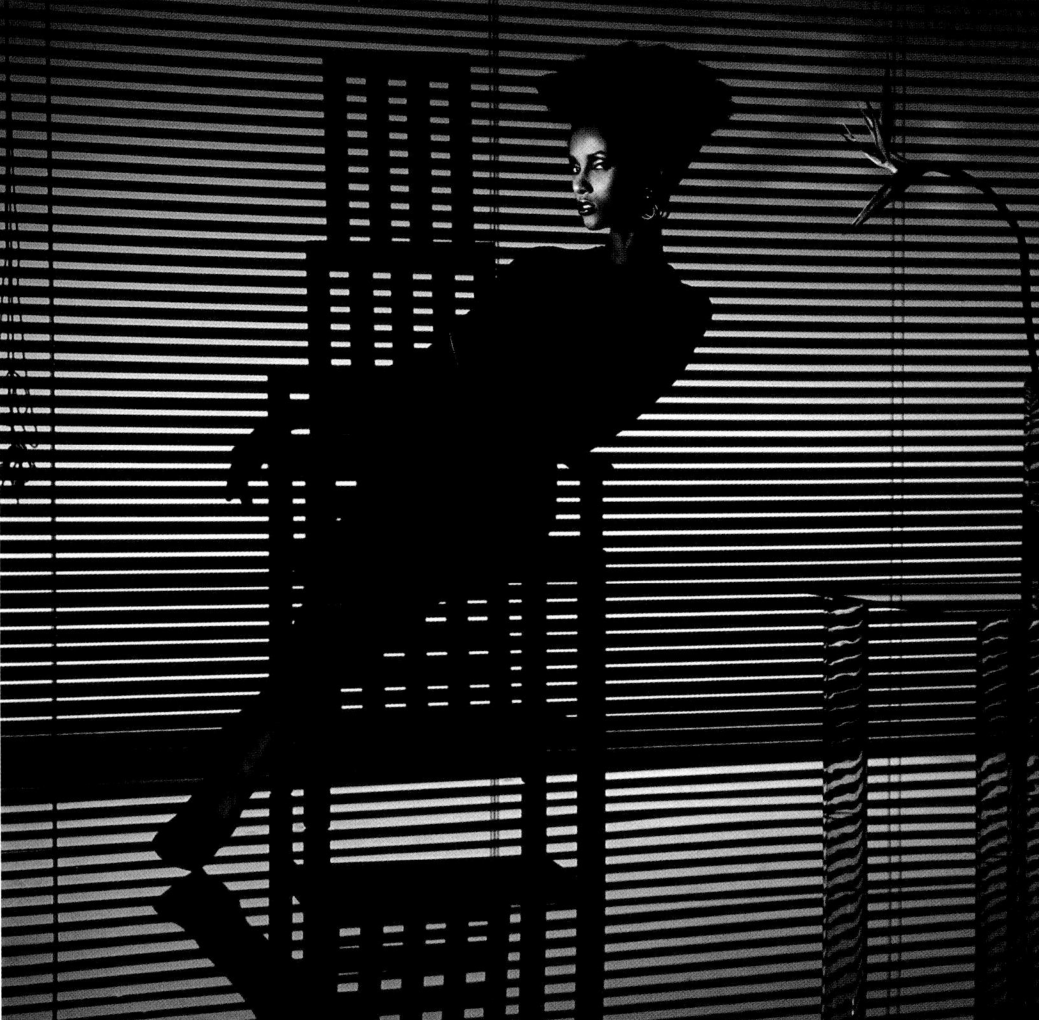

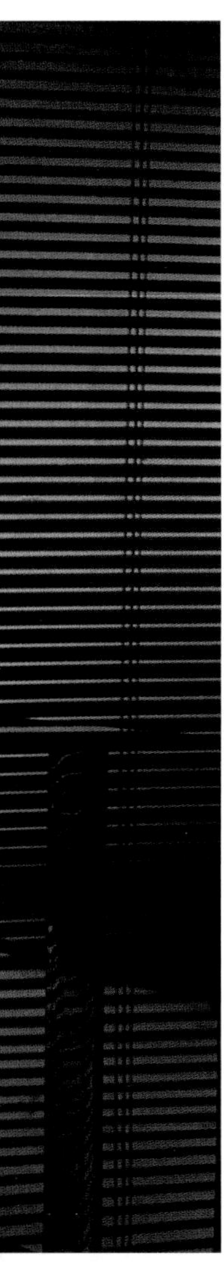

IMAN (b.1955)
John Swannell, 1984
Inkjet print, 393 x 497mm
NPG x134781

MADONNA (b.1958)

Eric Watson, 1984

Gelatin silver print,

286 x 395mm

NPG x125306

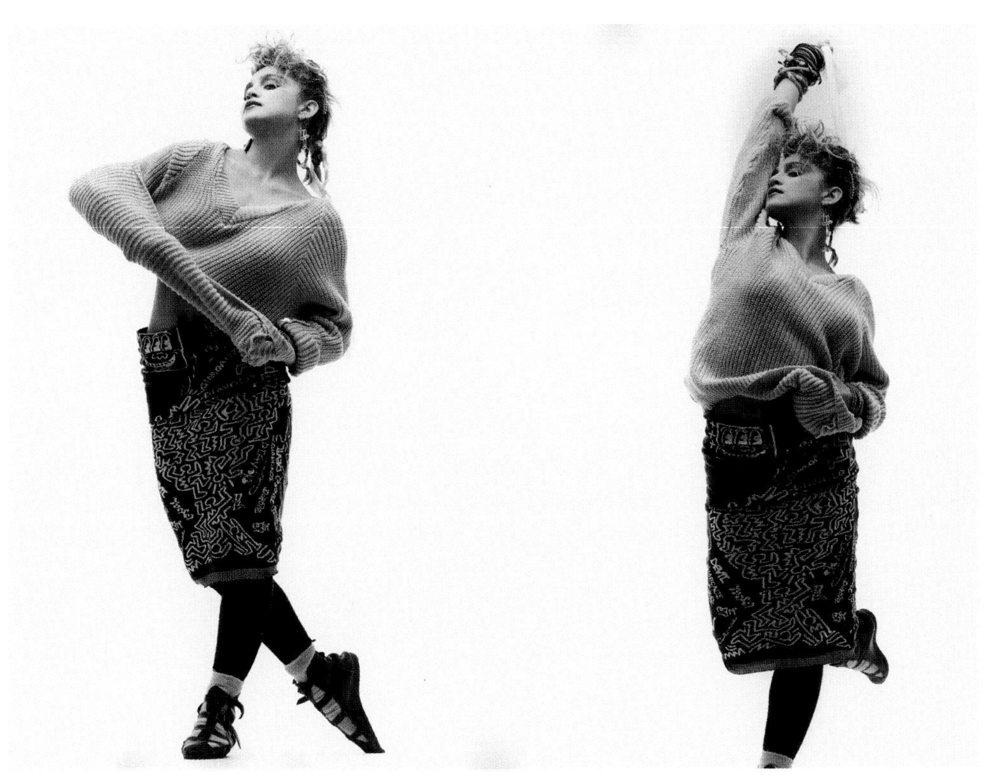

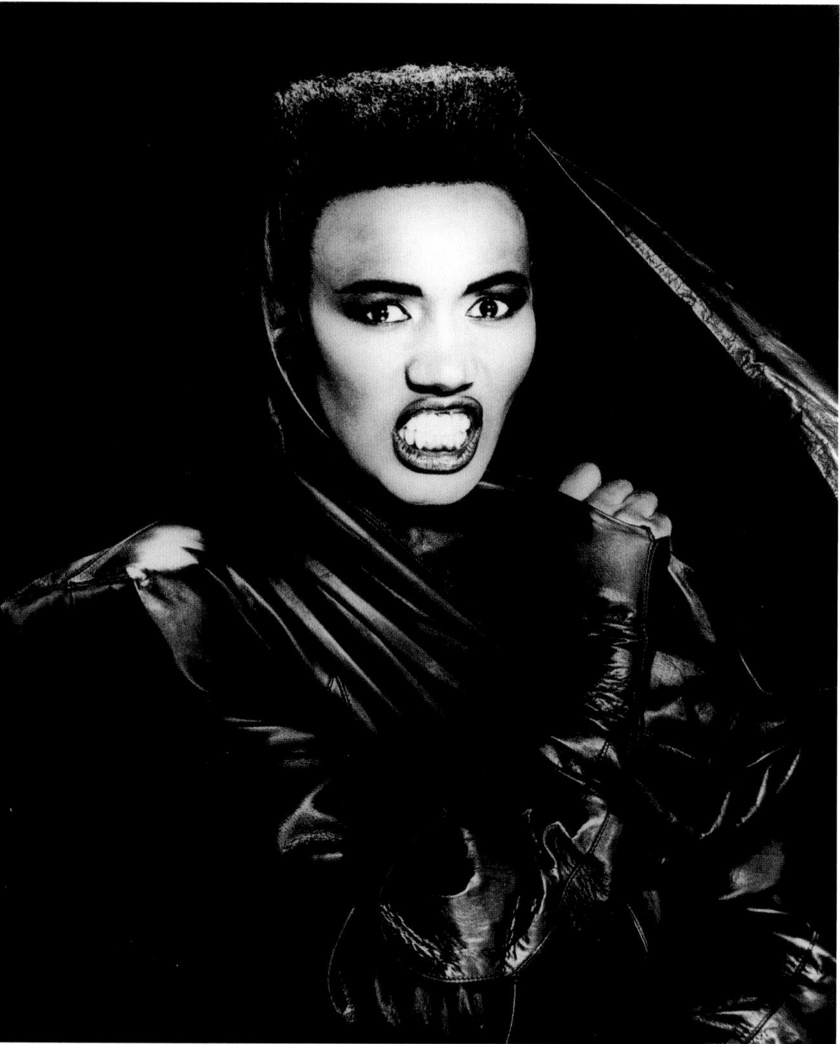

GRACE JONES (b.1948)
John Swannell, 1989
Inkjet print, 492 x 394mm
NPG x87596

VICTORIA BECKHAM (b.1975)
and DAVID BECKHAM (b.1975)
(*David and Victoria, Manchester 1998, No.3*)
Juergen Teller, 1998
Chromogenic print, 880 x 1280mm
NPG x199693

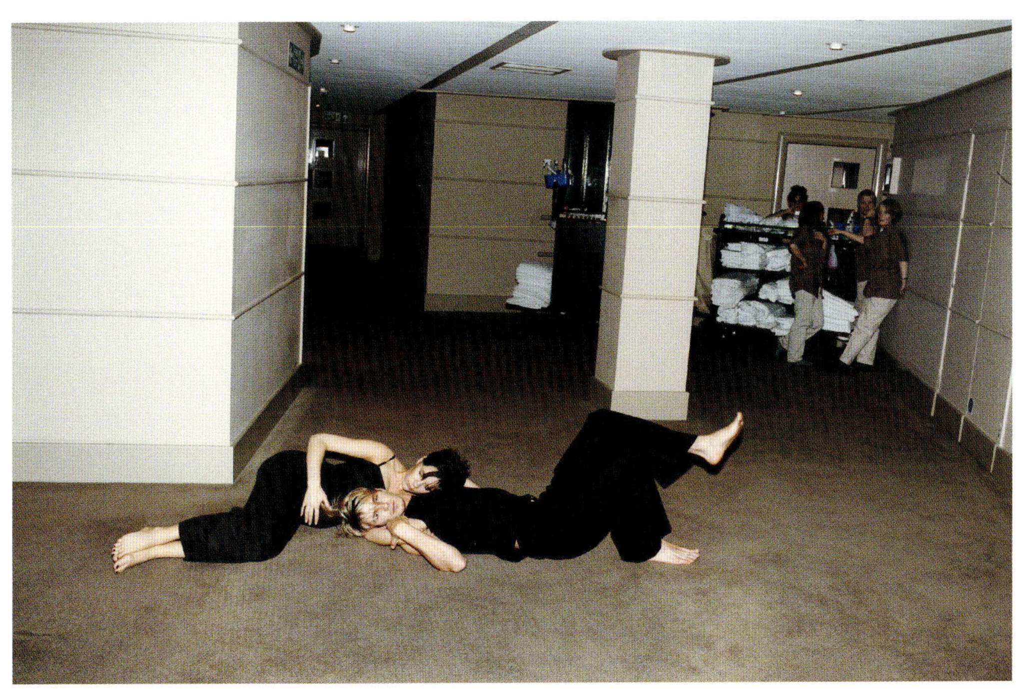

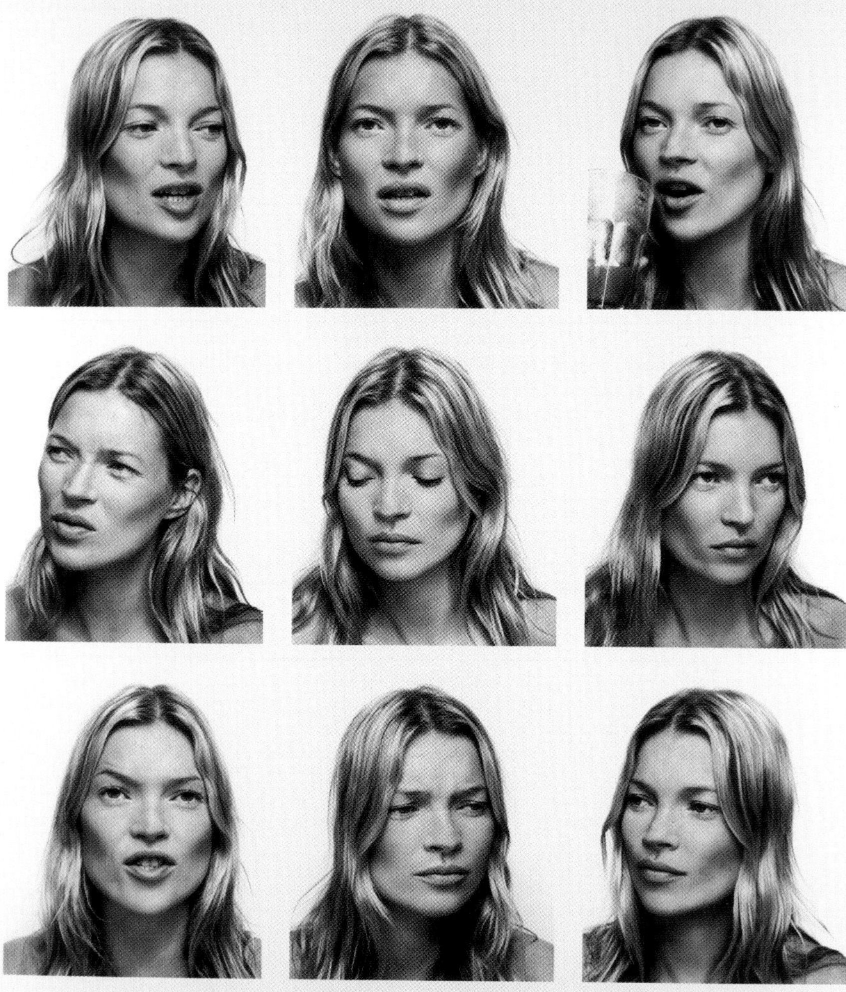

KATE MOSS (b.1974)
Corinne Day, 2006
Gelatin silver print, 1510 x 1305mm
NPG P1274

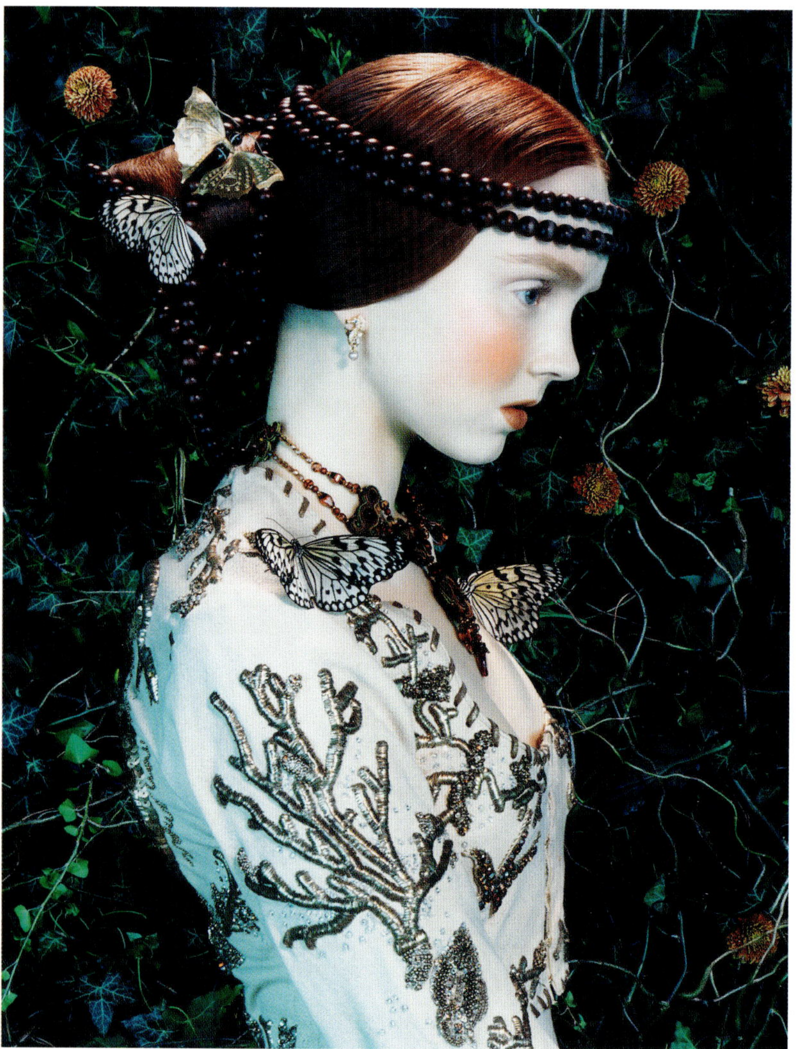

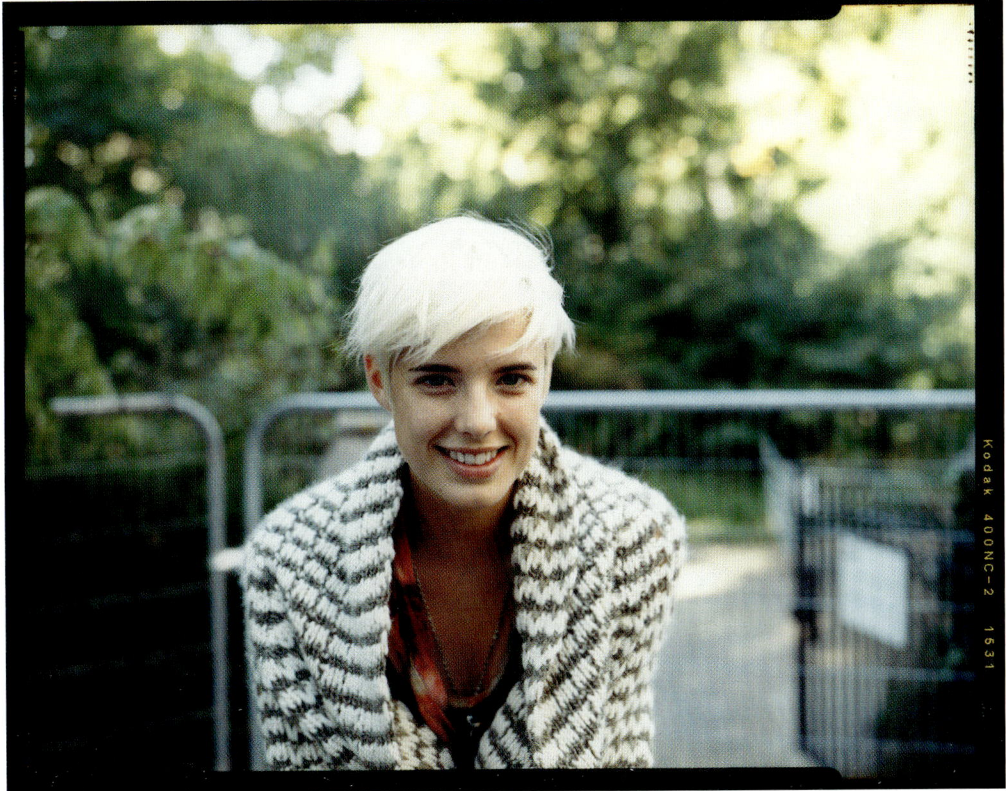

LILY COLE (b.1987) (*Like a Painting*)

Miles Aldridge, 2005

Digital chromogenic print, 506 x 380mm

NPG x131994

AGYNESS DEYN (b.1983)

Anna Bauer, 2007

Chromogenic contact print, 93 x 123mm

NPG x131797

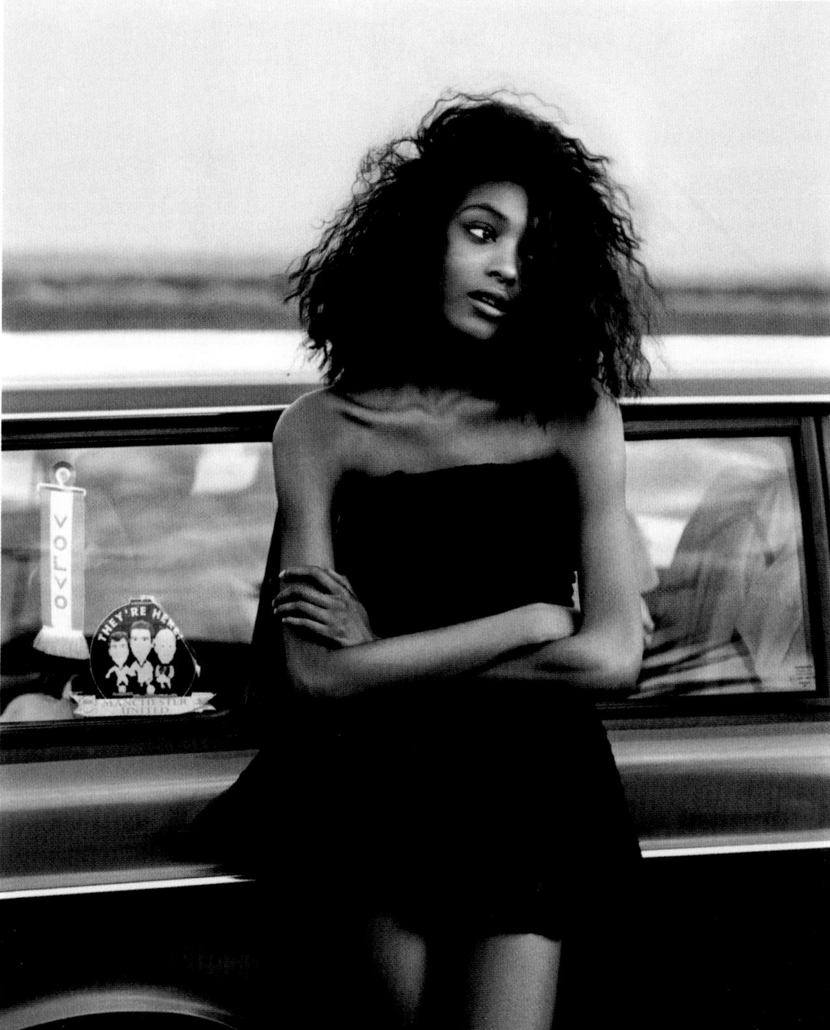

VOLVO
THEY'RE HERE
MANCHESTER UNITED

JOURDAN DUNN (b.1990)
Alasdair McLellan, 2008
Chromogenic print, 455 x 360mm
NPG x132440

NAOMI CAMPBELL (b.1970)

Simon Frederick, 2016

Inkjet print, 420 x 295mm

NPG P2035

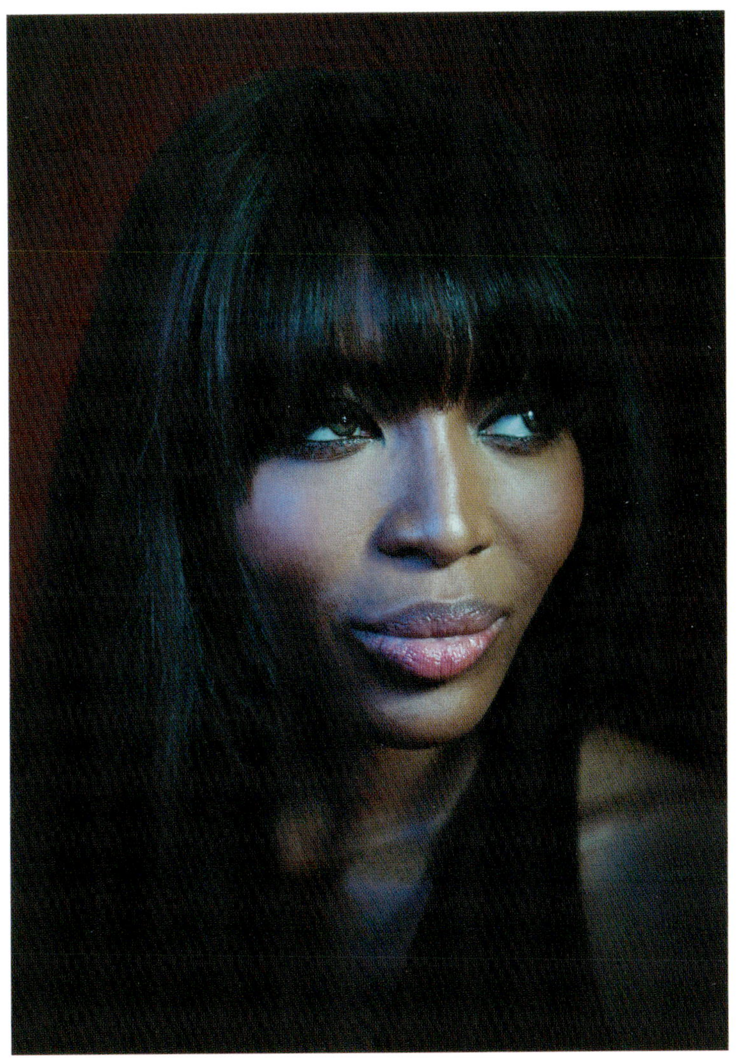

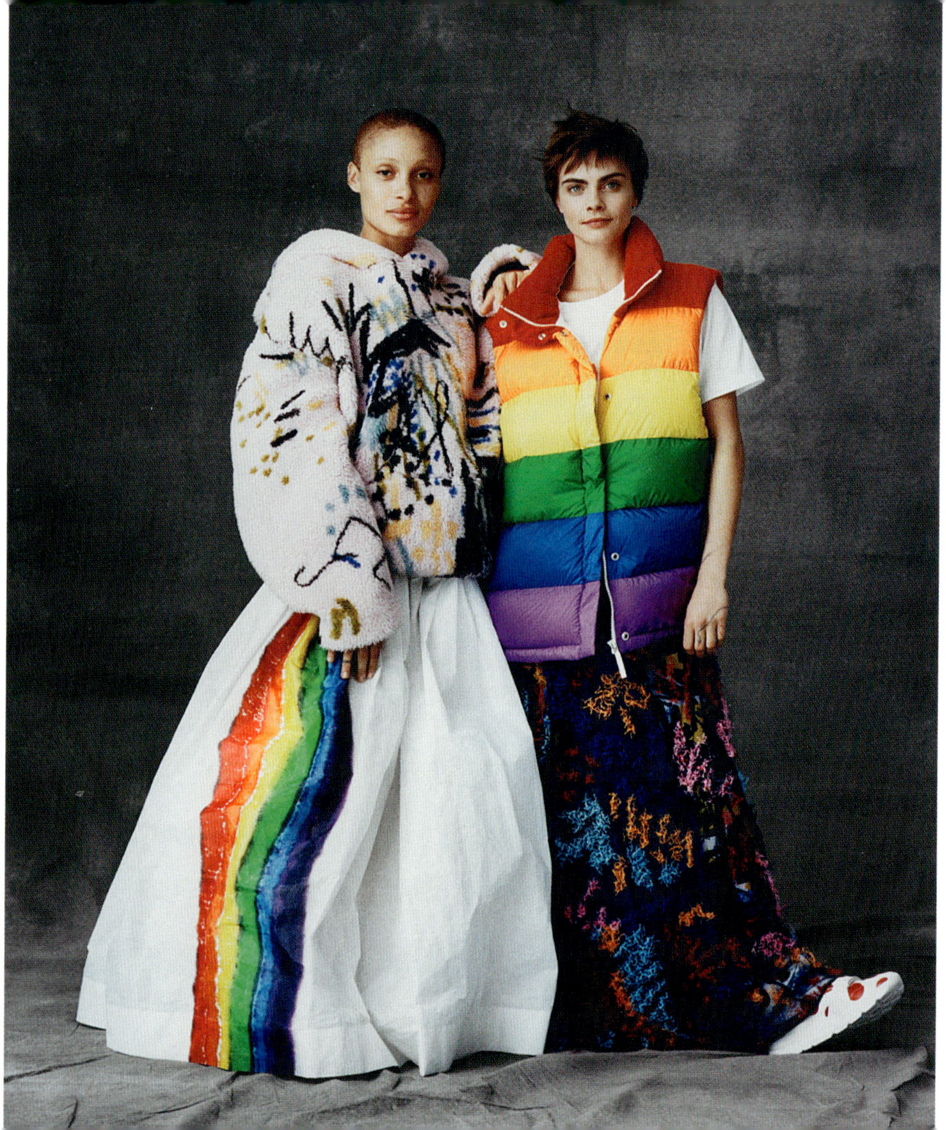

ADWOA ABOAH (b.1992) and
CARA DELEVINGNE (b.1992)
Paul Wetherell, 2018
Inkjet print, 455 x 355mm
NPG x200721

Renowned for their outspoken social
activism, the prominent fashion models
and friends Adwoa Aboah and Cara
Delevingne suitably opened and closed
Christopher Bailey's (b.1972) final runway
show for Burberry in 2018. Celebrating
Bailey's transformative tenure as designer
and Chief Executive Officer for the
brand, his bold collection demonstrated
retro streetwear influences and relaxed
glamour, as seen in Aboah's oversized
graffiti-print hoodie and casual full skirt,
and Delevingne's padded gilet and
polka-dot trainers. The recurring rainbow
motif in the collection paid homage to
the LGBTQ community – Bailey was
notably the first openly gay executive
among FTSE 100 corporations. Published
in *Vogue* in 2018, this photograph is from a
series taken by Paul Wetherell honouring
Bailey's legacy.

PICTURE CREDITS

Commissioned; made possible by J.P. Morgan through the Fund for New Commissions, 2014; p.71, p.171 © Simon Frederick/National Portrait Gallery, London. Given by Simon Frederick with support from Oath, 2017; p.72 © Benjamin McMahon; p.75 © Catherine Opie, courtesy of Regen Projects, Los Angeles and Thomas Dane Gallery, London. Purchased with support from Ivor Braka, 2018; p.88, p.97, p.101, p.129 © William Hustler and Georgina Hustler/National Portrait Gallery, London. Given by the photographer's sister, Susan Morton, 1976; p.91 © estate of Doris Clare Zinkeisen; p.92 © reserved; collection National Portrait Gallery, London. Given by the sitter's sister, Myra Verney, 1992; p.95, p.126 © Yevonde Portrait Archive. Given by Madame Yevonde, 1971; p.106 © Steve Hiett; p.108 © James Barnor; p.111 © Eve Arnold/Magnum Photos; p.112 © Horace Ové/National Portrait Gallery, London; p.114–15 © Elaine Constantine @ IndustryArt. Given by Elaine Constantine, 2007; p.116 © Olivia Rose; p.119 © Miles Aldridge. Given by Miles Aldridge, 2019; p.134 © Houghton Library, Harvard University; p.135 © The Cecil Beaton Studio Archive at Sotheby's. Given by Sir Cecil Beaton, 1968; p.137 © Lewis Morley/National Science & Media Museum/Science & Society Picture Library. Given by Lewis Morley, 1997; p.138 © David Bailey; p.141 © Robert Whitaker. Purchased with help from Gift Aid visitor ticket donations, 2009; p.142 © estate of Ronald Traeger; p.145 Photograph by Gered Mankowitz © Bowstir Ltd 2018/mankowitz.com; p.146 Patrick Lichfield. Given by Thomas Patrick John Anson, 5th Earl of Lichfield, 2003 in conjunction with the exhibition 'Lichfield: the early years 1962–1982'; p.149 © Terry O'Neill/Iconic Images. Given by Terry O'Neill, 2003; p.150 Photo Duffy © Duffy Archive & The David Bowie Archive™; p.153 © David Gwinnutt/National Portrait Gallery, London; p.156–7 © John Swannell/Camera Press. Given by John Swannell, 2011; p.159 © Eugene and Willa Watson/National Portrait Gallery, London; p.160 © John Swannell/Camera Press. Given by John Swannell, 1998; p.163 © Juergen Teller, All rights reserved. Given by Juergen Teller, 2016; p.164 © Estate of Corinne Day/Commissioned by the National Portrait Gallery, London/trunkarchive.com. Commissioned, 2007; p.166 © Miles Aldridge. Given by Miles Aldridge, 2008; p.167 © Anna Bauer. Given by Anna Bauer, 2008; p.168 © Alasdair McLellan/Art Partner. Given by Alasdair McLellan, 2009.

Additional commissioning and acquisition information for images © National Portrait Gallery, London:

p.9 Bequeathed by the estate of Francis Goodman, 1989; p.13 Acquired Victoria & Albert Museum, 1998; pp.22–3 Given by John Culme, 1996; p.28 Bequeathed by Marie Anita Gay (née Arnheim), 2003; p.54 Commissioned as part of the First Prize, 1997 BP Portrait Award, 1998; p.77 Given by Emery Walker Ltd, 1956; p.78 Bequeathed by the sitter's son, Ernest Svend David Goldschmidt, 1951; p.80 Purchased with help from the Art Fund and the National Lottery Heritage Fund, 2002; p.81 Bequeathed by Rolf, Baron Cederström, 1948; p.82 Given by the photographer's son, Cavendish Morton, 1991; p.83 Given by Arthur Myers Smith, 1926; p.85 Given by The Medici Society Ltd, 1910; p.86 Given by John Morton Morris, 2004; p.87 Given by Bassano & Vandyk Studios, 1974; p.96 Bequeathed by the estate of Francis Goodman, 1989; p.98 Given by the photographer's sister, Susan Morton, 1976; p.105 Given by the sitter and artist, Gluck (Hannah Gluckstein), 1973; p.123, p.125 Bequeathed by Patrick O'Connor, 2010; p.130 Transferred from Evening Standard Library, 1983; p.154 Commissioned, 1981.

Published in Great Britain by National Portrait Gallery
Publications, St Martin's Place, London WC2H 0HE

For a complete catalogue of current publications, please visit
our website at www.npg.org.uk/publications

ISBN 978 1 85514 737 9

A catalogue record for this book is available from
the British Library.

10 9 8 7 6 5 4 3 2 1

Head of Commercial: Anna Starling
Publishing Manager: Kara Green
Production Manager: Ruth Müller-Wirth
Project Editor: Tijana Todorinovic
Designer: Peter Dawson, Alice Kennedy-Owen, gradedesign.com

Caption texts written jointly by Georgia Atienza, Clare
Freestone, Sabina Jaskot-Gill, Grace Lee, Georgina Mind and
Constantia Nicolaides.

Printed in Italy

Notes on style conventions

Dimensions expressed height x width (mm), apart from
archive negatives. The given titles of the portraits are shown
italicised in brackets after the sitter's name; where the sitter's
name is not shown, the given title of the work appears in
roman.

Acknowledgements

The National Portrait Gallery Collection has grown through
the generosity of many institutions, families and individuals
who have donated important works. Equally important has
been the support over many decades of the Art Fund (formerly
known as the National Art Collections Fund), and in more
recent years of the National Heritage Memorial Fund and the
Heritage Lottery Fund. The Gallery's own Portrait Fund has
become increasingly significant, and the National Portrait Gallery
is very grateful to all those who have supported the Fund as
well as the public campaigns to acquire particular portraits.